THE CLASSY HUSTLE

DISCLAIMER

The information provided in this book is for informational purposes only and is not intended to be a source of advice or analysis with respect to the material presented. The information and/or documents contained in this book do not constitute legal, tax or financial advice and should never be used without first consulting with legal, tax, and financial professionals to determine what may be best for your individual needs.

The publisher and the author do not make any guarantee or other promise as to any results that may be obtained from using the content of this book. You should never make any legal, tax or financial decisions without first consulting with your own legal, tax and financial professionals and conducting your own research and due diligence. To the maximum extent permitted by law, the publisher and the author disclaim any and all liability in the event any information, commentary, analysis, opinions, advice and/or recommendations contained in this book prove to be inaccurate, incomplete or unreliable, or result in any business, legal, tax, financial or other losses.

Content contained or made available through this book is not intended to and does not constitute legal, tax, or financial advice and no attorney-client relationship is formed. The publisher and the author are providing this book and its contents on an "as is" basis. Your use of the information in this book is at your own risk.

THE CLASSY HUSTLE

By Tessa Boyd

First edition October 2020

Front cover image by Scott Watt of Scott Watt Photography
Book design by Business Marketing Engine

ISBN 978-1-7352339-0-1 (paperback)
ISBN 978-1-7352339-9-4 (hardcover)
ISBN 978-1-7352339-1-8 (ebook)
ISBN 978-1-7352339-2-5 (audiobook)

Tessa E. Boyd
522 S. Hunt Club Blvd. Suite 365
Apopka, FL 32703

TABLE OF CONTENTS

Foreword
Preface
Introduction - *Rufus Troy Alexander*

PREFACE

I woke up, did my devotions and prepared for my day. I pulled the Murphy bed from off the floor and put it back where it spends the day — in the cabinet. I hid the fact that I lived in the same space as my business. Closing the cabinet doors indicated that my living space no longer existed. The transition from the living space to my work space is complete when I put the massage tables back in their place. My place then looked like a skincare school instead of my home. My day could then begin. My regular routine included showering and putting on my lounge wear to walk down the hallway. The hallway leads to where my "walk-in closet" is located. Some people would call my walk-in closet a storage unit, but I liked the term, "walk-in closet" better. I picked out my clothes for the day, looked in my full-length mirror to make sure that I was looking my best. I walked out of my closet and went back down the hallway to my work space. I always ate a light breakfast that had no defining odor to avoid being caught by someone who might ask the dreaded question "Do you live here?" I always wanted to avoid this question. I cringed every time I heard it.

The carpet on my floor created such a cozy environment that my school felt like it was a second home to anyone who came in. People always wanted to know if I lived in my living/work suite. I wanted to answer honestly, but did not want to risk the judgement that followed. I also did not want to risk the Cosmetology Board finding out. I would answer in various ways, "I could live here as it is a living/work space". Other times, I would answer that I live in the building. No matter how I answered, I seldom shared with anyone that I actually lived in my business space.

The struggles that came along with living in my business space for three-and-a-half years were humbling. My dreams and visions comforted me. I loved hearing about my students' and friends' adventures of international travel. I longed for the day that I too would be able to travel for business and for pleasure.

Fast forward eight years to December, 2019. I woke up, did my devotions and prepared for my day while getting ready for my vacation to Dubai, UAE. I had taken 13 days off from my business so my husband and I could go on an adventure of a lifetime. We visited France, Czech Republic, UAE, Oman and Russia over the course of 11 days.

I am amazed that in eight short years I was able to travel and experience the world. I no longer had to live vicariously through the experiences of my friends and students. I had my own experiences and memories to hold on to.

What if I never started my business? What if the ideas stayed in my mind and I never followed through on them? I know without a shadow of a doubt that I would have had several corporate jobs. I also know that I most likely would be making six figures from one of those jobs. With all of the apparent successes, I would have still felt limited in what I was capable of doing. Had I stayed working in the corporate world, these limitations would have caused me grief, frustration and unhappiness.

You never know how far your business can take you until you begin. Internationally renowned author and speaker, Wayne Dyer says, "Begin with the end in mind. Start with the end outcome and work backward to make your dream possible." Those words have always resonated with and inspired me, and I hope they do the same for you. My hope is that after you read this book, you are able to live your dream of starting your own business.

"The Classy Hustle" was created from my desire of owning my own business even though I had limited resources. At the time, I was single, divorced and living in a city 1,000 miles away from my immediate family members. I wanted to start a business that was sustainable and be able to tell my story in a way that was ethical, upright and a bit humorous. I hope that you enjoy reading this book as much as I enjoyed writing it. This book chronicles my journey to entrepreneurship.

INTRODUCTION

What we have here is a book but not a story. It's just a glimpse of someone's life. We all go through life. We all know life can't always be fully-controlled by the person living it. Life has it's unexpected events and unexpected twist and turns, ups and downs, highs and lows. You get what I'm saying. Knowing this is life and what comes with it, we have to decide if we're going to let it control us and not make something of ourselves, OR, and this is a big OR, we have to decide to acknowledge the worst parts that have occurred and that will occur in our lives. Once we acknowledge them, we can be upset in the moment, but you just have to keep moving forward. Tessa is someone who, despite having an option to quit, kept moving forward.

I've had the pleasure of watching the life of my sister evolve. Since we're several years apart in age, she's played a big role in raising me. She's been someone who I can always get an honest opinion from. She's that person who is unable to sugar-coat anything, mainly because life doesn't sugar-coat anything. This book is basically like that, too: a life not sugar-coated. That could've also been the title for this book. Hmmm.

I've seen my sister hurt, cry, be mad, be sad, accomplish goals, exceed goals all while carrying herself with class. She's truly an amazing person who deserves all she has because none of it was given to her — it was all hustled with class. Don't take my word for it. Just continue turning the pages to see what I mean!

God Bless, *Rufus Troy Alexander*

1 | BIRTHED FROM PAIN

Working in corporate America quickly helped me to identify the areas I liked and showed me the areas I did not like. I loved the fact of knowing how much money I was going to make every two weeks. I enjoyed the security and comfort of having a salary and benefits. I did not like the moments when I questioned my work ethic based on the perception others had of me.

The process of growing in my career by getting promoted came fairly easy. I worked hard and expected to make more money, as money was always a motivating factor. I thought that if I worked hard and showed upper management my strong work ethic that promotion and praise should immediately follow.

This was not the case for me. After years of trying to fit in, a situation that confirmed I was a misfit would always present itself. The last situation I encountered like this landed me on a green bench contemplating my next move in life. I knew that this next move would change the trajectory of my life. Therefore, it had to be well-thought-out.

A SUDDEN SHIFT
After eight months of being in the classroom full time, a sudden shift took place. Management told me that I

could either work part-time hours as an adjunct skin-care instructor or I could apply for the Director of Education position. While both options sounded promising, I did not want to work part-time because it would force me to work a second job. I did not want to apply for the director of education position and have to go back into full-time management. I wanted to stay right where I was for as long as I could, working 34 hours a week as a skincare instructor.

The choice of me teaching 34 hours a week was no longer an option for me. The lack of appealing choices led me to apply for the director of education position even though there had been five previous directors over the past five years. The hiring manager made it crystal clear that it was incredibly important that they select and hire the right person, otherwise she and her entire team would be fired. I already felt extreme pressure to perform if I were to be the one chosen for the position.

After four weeks of deliberation, I was selected for the position. After I was hired, they made a grand announcement, and I was orientated into the world of education. The first order of business was to fire some tenured professors, as the curriculum had changed. I was also told that I would need to grow the student population and launch the new curriculum.

I questioned my ability to perform my job. I had never managed men before, and I was in a position where I had to manage men my father's age. Since I never had to do this before, I knew that I needed the help of a mentor. For me to be successful in this role, I needed grooming.

My first order of business was to fire tenured professors, one who was my father's age. He had white hair, was bearded and was loved by everyone. I thought calling him on a Saturday morning would soften the blow, as I had procrastinated firing him for weeks. I told him that we were doing away with the program that he was teaching, effective immediately. His voice raised and he asked me if I was firing him. He was direct in his questioning, and I was trying to be passive in my approach. My hands were sweating and my voice was quivering. But, I was able to give him an affirmative answer. Meanwhile, as I looked at myself through the reflection of a mirrored door, I realized that I had done it. I terminated my first employee even though I had been scared to do it.

After that phone call, I called my mentor to receive solace. She comforted me and reassured me that this was the most difficult part of managing people and that it would get easier. This part of the job is still one of the hardest tasks for me to do, but I will do it without hesitation.

I accomplished some wonderful things within three years. The student population grew by thirty percent. I implemented a new curriculum, grew my faculty to over 38 employees and increased the completion rate. Because of these accomplishments, I was next in line for a promotion. The education group I worked for was acquiring new colleges and I was asked to open the new campus in Texas. I started looking for apartments and checking out the demographics of the state.

I had told several coworkers that I would be relocating to Texas to open up the brand new campus. I was looking forward to the official announcement about my upcoming relocation during a conference call with the entire management team. Our COO began discussing the new school openings. He said he was excited to announce that someone else would be opening up the new campus in Texas. I paused for a moment wondering why he forgot to say my name. Then, it suddenly dawned on me that it was because I was not chosen to go. My heart sank, tears filled my eyes, and I was embarrassed.

At that moment, I made a decision to leave the scene. I stood up from my desk, walked out of my office, down the hallway to the nearest exit. I walked down the stairs through the door. It took everything within me to hold back the tears and compose myself. I walked through the parking lot and sat on a green bench.

CHANGING THE TRAJECTORY OF MY LIFE

This green bench encounter changed the trajectory of my life. The conversation I had with myself was a turning point. Having experienced a divorce, this type of relationship was familiar to me. I equated my work relationships to being in a toxic, volatile marriage. It represented the uncertainties of knowing where one can stand with an ex-spouse. When you do something good, you are praised, but as soon as you do something the person doesn't agree with, you are berated. I had a toxic and unhealthy relationship with my employer that needed to change. I was responsible for allowing them to treat me in this manner. I had more power than I realized and was giving my power away. This day marked the day everything was going to change.

I decided to rip the bandaid off of my wound, believe in myself and make some entrepreneurial moves. Within three weeks of the conference call and my bench encounter, I incorporated my business. I scheduled an appointment to meet with a leasing agent about the living/work space unit I had been interested in. I even went as far as bringing boxes into my office to start packing. While I didn't know where I was going, I knew that I would be leaving my corporate job soon.

Some of my faculty started asking me what the boxes were for. I said that my office needed decluttering and that I was getting prepared to leave when the time came. I got to the point where I hated coming into the office. I felt like my soul left that place after that conference call. I was merely existing but not living. My face began to show my apathy, and there was little I could do to hide it.

The weeks leading to my separation were dramatic. I came into work on a Monday morning and did my usual walk through the campus. The energy was different. The hallways felt tense and the instructors looked scared. I wished good morning to people as I always did, and one faculty member whispered to me that a corporate team member was on campus. He said that she was hiding in the hallway making observations. I didn't know if I should laugh at the foolishness or be afraid. I decided to be fearless. My office was already packed and I was ready to go.

I finally saw the corporate manager hiding in the hallway and greeted her with a good morning. She responded the same. She asked me about my schedule for the week and asked if she could meet with me on Wednesday. I agreed to the meeting. When Wednesday came, she met me in my office and made a call to another corporate manager. She said that she wanted to go over my job description. She went through each bullet point to see if each task was being performed. She found herself answering yes to every bullet point. It was obvious that I was doing my job and that she was searching for errors in my performance and that I was being set up. To her dismay, she was unable to find any deficiencies.

After she read the entire job description, she paused. She then asked the other corporate team member on the call for comments. Within minutes, the conversation escalated to a shocking level of anger. He began to holler at me about a comment I made on one of our conference calls. My anger began to match his and the lioness in me began to roar. I asked him who he thought he was talking to like that. When he saw that I wasn't afraid, he backed down a little but still continued to show frustration toward me.

It became obvious that I was the topic of discussion and the target of the corporate team. They were trying to figure out a way to break me and fire me. It was not going to happen without a fight. The policies for the education group were changing, and I was being asked to compromise my integrity. I voiced my concern on a call by stating that I was having ethical dilemmas in what they were asking me to do. As a result, I was viewed by the corporate team as being insubordinate. In hindsight, I should have requested a meeting with them to discuss my concerns.

As more concerns came up, I was being called into more meetings. The meetings became senseless, with a bunch of he said/she said accusations with no concrete evidence. The meetings went on from that Wednesday until the following Friday. The conversations during meetings began to shift to where people were saying outright lies about my character. I continued to take my stance but was growing weary. I did not know how much more I could take before losing it, but I was determined to not break.

My final meeting on Friday was pre-orchestrated by the management team. Our seating arrangement was strategically placed. I was seated next to the corporate manager who was trying to fire me. The instructor who was called into the office sat next to me, closest to the door. The tension in the room was so thick it is palpable. The corporate manager began the meeting with statements. There is not much of a conversation but more of a one-way lecture. She talked and we listened. When the instructor tried to talk, his comments were not heard. After several minutes of her interrupting him, I asked on his behalf if he could speak without interruption. She was infuriated by my request and viewed me as being insubordinate.

The teacher asked if he could step out to compose himself but was denied. I interjected and told him that he could leave. Upon his exit, I was left with my immediate supervisor and the woman from the corporate office. She told me to go home. I asked her why I was being asked to leave and her answer was simply because she said so. This answer was not acceptable to me, so I continued to probe. As she continued to tell me to go home, I continued to tell her to go home. This banter went back and forth until finally my direct supervisor told me to leave. I agreed to leave as long as she was willing to escort me out of the building. I did not think it would be a good idea for the corporate manager to escort me out. My manager agreed, and some of my last words to her were "please don't let them lie on me." I called human resources to file a complaint and was told that I was suspended with pay until the investigation was completed.

I drove away knowing in my heart that I would not be returning. I did not want to be alone, so I called my mentor. She suggested that I come to her house. I drove to her house to debrief and calm down. Once she heard what I had to say, she asked me what outcome I wanted. I paused for a moment to gather my thoughts. It was an interesting question because I was so focused on winning that I did not know what the fight was. After pausing to gather my thoughts, I told her that I did not want to go back but I did not want to struggle financially after leaving.

The investigation went on for about two weeks. During this time, I focused on sleeping in and working out in a late-morning class. I wanted to relax and enjoy not being in a fight. I wanted peace and to feel normal again. I was tired of being falsely accused. After waiting for a couple of weeks, I finally received the phone call from upper management that I had been waiting for. There were two corporate big-wigs on the call with me. We were cordial to each other, but I could hear in the gentleman's voice that he was struggling to find the right words. There was some disappointment and lots of caution in his voice. The phone call was exactly what I wanted to hear. Finally, after four months of leaving my corporate job, my dream of owning and running a skincare school came to fruition!

After separating from my job, I had some big-girl decisions to make concerning my finances and starting my business. I chose to use all of my resources to invest in myself and my business. I chose my business more than my own comforts. The studio suite I leased was considered both a living and working space, so I was going to do just that. I was going to live on one side and work on the other.

I ended up occupying the living/work space for three-and-a-half years. I like to say that I lived as if I did not live there. One of my costliest initial investments was purchasing a walnut-colored Murphy bed that looked like a bookcase. The wall-bed style had accordion-style double doors that opened outward. This was where my queen-size mattress was hidden. Every evening after classes were done, I moved the massage tables to allow room for my bed to come down from the wall. There was a sense of comfort I would get from pulling my mattress out of the wall down to the floor. I had a way of jumping into my bed like I was escaping the outer world even if just for a few hours of rest.

Kevin Trudeau states in his audio reading, "Your Wish is Your Command, How to Manifest Your Desires" that you will not be balanced when you first begin to birth a vision, and being balanced was something I was not. I dreamed about my school day and night and could not escape it for three-and-a-half years. At night, while lying in my bed, I would look to the ceiling and around the school and dream about it growing. I dreamed about the students who would be coming. I dreamed about expanding and the next suite I was going to acquire. I dreamed incessantly.

Near the end of my third year of living in the same space where my business was, my mother had an intervention call with me. She expressed her concern about my mental state due to my combined living and working space. She was concerned about me living within the small confines of 960 square feet for such a long period of time. She explained her concern over my never being able to escape it. But, actually I did. When the school had its first Saturday class from 8:30 a.m. to 5:00 p.m., I would get in my car and drive around the block for about 10 minutes, or until I felt like I was leaving work. Then, I would drive right back to my living/work space. But, walking into the space at this time was different because I was now coming home. To solidify that I was home, my ritual included rearranging the tables and massage beds and embracing my living quarters. On the weekends, I would keep my bed down the entire time so that I could feel like I was at home.

Living there like I did not really live there required some serious skills. I would only cook on Saturday evening through Sunday afternoon so that the cooking aromas would be out by Monday's work day. I mastered knowing which foods left lingering smells. Cooking collard greens was a no-no! I also had a specific way of hiding my pots and pans. My studio suite was equipped with a gourmet kitchen. I hid my silverware, plates, pots and pans in the broiler part of the oven. I leased two storage spaces, one had the walk-in closet and the other was where I stored all of my personal possessions. My entire life, including my business, occupied about 960 square feet and I could not have been happier. I stayed focused on what mattered most, and I was living out the American Dream!

I had my normal morning routine down to a science. It required me showering in my suite, putting on loungewear and walking to my walk-in closet, the storage space. One morning, I walked into my walk-in closet as one of my neighbors was walking past with her dog. I picked out my wardrobe for the day and changed into my dress pants, blouse and heels. I pranced out of the closet and began walking toward my studio. This same neighbor must have finished her walk with her dog at the same time as me. She walked past and we spoke again but this time she asked if I lived in the storage space. I was immediately agitated and felt exposed but I was able to gather my thoughts and pleasantly reply that I didn't as I continued prancing down the hallway.

CAUGHT!

I started my venture by teaching evening classes from 6-10 p.m. Monday through Thursday. Then started adding on daytime classes that met from 9 a.m.-1 p.m. After the last student left, I would quickly transition the workspace back into my living space. At times, I would transition so quickly that I would forget to lock the front door. One morning, I did my normal routine of showering and putting on lounge gear to walk to my walk-in closet. As I was about to put on my loungewear, I heard the front door open up and a warm, friendly voice followed. I wanted to scream, "noooooo" but could not because the person was already inside looking directly at me, as I was wearing nothing but my bra and panties.

I was exposed. She immediately felt my embarrassment and told me to give her a hug. No other words followed for a few moments. She was my banker, whom I once asked for a business loan. While I was denied the loan, we remained good friends. She was in the area and wanted to stop by to see my establishment. What she saw was more than my establishment. She saw my determination and drive to do whatever it took to reach my goals. She actually was impressed with the sacrifice I made and vowed to help me in whatever capacity she could. To date, she has helped me start my first business money market account. She was instrumental in getting me a business line of credit for $50,000 and she continues to help me however she can.

GETTING HELP ALONG THE WAY

Several people will help you along the way. She and another business banker tried to get me approved for a small business loan. I thought because I was female and minority, I could easily get approved for a startup loan. But, to get a loan, you must already have money or collateral. Since I had no money, it forced me to get extremely creative on how I was going to finance my business. The two bankers were impressed with the business plan I presented and believed in my vision. Even with these plusses, I was unable to qualify for a small business loan.

The bankers continued supporting me by coming to the school's student spa. They received facials services from our students. Upon their arrival to their appointments, I greeted them with a smile and said, "Hello to the ladies who didn't approve me for a loan". The one banker quickly pointed out that they are also the ladies I didn't owe money to. That sentiment resonated with me and allowed me to put things into perspective. I owed no one any money except me.

2 | LETTING GO OF LIMITING BELIEFS

MINDSET

I was listening to a podcast by a speaker who was telling his story about nearly being evicted. The point he was driving home was that although he knew how to make money, he didn't know how to keep it. Somehow, he kept finding himself losing all the money he made. He finally addressed his issue of having the wrong mindset toward money. His story represents the story of many people who have unhealthy views about money. This also was one of my biggest fears I had of becoming successful.

Many people know how to make money but do not know how to keep money. They find themselves broke in retirement even after having a successful career for years. The average person makes over $1 million dollars over a lifetime. Despite this fact, many people do not have more than $100,000 in savings for retirement. Many people feel that they have to spend everything they have for fear of losing their money.

If given the opportunity, I would save my way to having millions instead of winning the lottery. Although this idea may seem surprising, this is how I look at it. Learning the value of saving one dollar at a time instills in me discipline and consistency. Winning a lump sum of money, makes it easy to spend it all because there was no work involved in getting it. Studies show that most lottery winners end up broke within a few years of winning. They also end up filing for bankruptcy.

I began to recognize that I saw illusions. People appeared successful but were losing their businesses and possessions. Because of my religious upbringing, I equated loss to the Devil attacking good people. After several therapy sessions, I realized that I was misplacing the blame. What I was blaming on the Devil was actually bad money management and lack of planning. People are living beyond their means. They are spending everything they have without saving money. There is an expression about failing to prepare meaning you are preparing to fail. Simply put, the reason for many failures is a lack of planning.

LETTING GO OF LIMITED BELIEFS

As I got closer to getting out of the fetal position my first year in business, I pondered the idea of whether I was scared of failure or scared of success. After days of deliberating, I realized that success scared me more than failure. I was more scared of losing everything once I obtained it. This thought caused me to dig a little deeper into self discovery. What did I see that caused me to fear losing things once I reached a point of success?

It was then that my memories went to my childhood. I saw people who were self-employed with businesses obtain success and lose things. I saw cars repossessed, homes foreclosed and government liens imposed on paychecks. As I thought back, I wondered if this would become me. I often addressed this fear in therapy sessions. It took several intense sessions to be able to answer some questions that convinced me that I was not those people:

1. Do you pay your taxes?

I was able to answer yes, and now I pay quarterly.

2. Do you have an honest CPA?

Yes. I worked with a reputable CPA firm that performs yearly reviews to ensure I am compliant.

3. Do you save money?

Yes, I am current on all my personal and business expenses and I save money.

4. Do you live within your means?

Absolutely.

After I was able to give an affirmative answer to all these questions, I realized that I had nothing to fear. It was also during this time that I questioned what people told me. I specifically questioned ways of obtaining wealth and obtaining it quickly. When I was growing up, my influencers had a "get rich quick" mentality. They were involved in multi-level marketing businesses (MLM), which many people refer to as pyramid schemes. I also saw these types of businesses abusing the people who were involved with them, so my viewpoint was tainted. I grew up seeing illusions. Whenever you can make a million dollars in six months, you can also lose a million dollars in three months.The more quickly people got money, the more quickly they lost it. Seeing this process in action created uncertainty for me.

Seeing things lost and repossessed created an inner unspoken fear inside me. I did not realize how many restrictions and limitations I placed on myself and my dreams. For years, I wanted to break free from these deep-rooted fears but I did not know how.

I was hearing sound bites of people's stories. It is easier for parents to give excuses to their children to justify certain behaviors by saying things like, "this business opportunity didn't work out" rather than acknowledging that they did not thoroughly research the venture. Simply put, it is easier to blame things on the Devil than to acknowledge that you did a poor job managing a company. Recognize unhealthy sound bites when you hear them. Understand that when they come up that there is likely more to the story than what is being told.

While you will not know everything, you can surround yourself with people who know more than you. It is wise to hire professional people who can help you make sound decisions. This is how you grow and you let go of the beliefs that limit you.

Here are some common areas where people tend to have limited beliefs:

1. *"I will never make more money."*
Making more money is reliant on knowing your worth. Many people make less money than they could because they do not ask for more money. They do not ask for more money because they do not feel worthy of having more money. A lot of people believe that if they ask for more money that they risk being terminated. The only thing your employer can tell you is "yes", "no", or "not now."

When I worked in corporate America, I had a team of instructors who had not received a pay increase in four years. So, when it came to be time for yearly reviews, no one really cared because they had nothing to look forward to. I saw their level of apathy. They knew that no matter how hard they worked that they would not be rewarded for their hard work. I knew I was their voice, so I went to upper management to ask for an increase on their behalf. Management's response was that the team members should be lucky to have a job. I was livid by that response. So in turn, I asked how she would feel if someone told her that she was not going to get an increase in pay and if she felt lucky to have a job. I awaited her response. There was none.

A few weeks later, I was on our conference call. I was told by the corporate team that I was being allotted a lump sum of money to distribute to my instructors. While it was not a lot, it was enough money for me to distribute something to each one of them. Their increase averaged around 1.5% of their hourly salary. While it was a small amount, this act let them know that they were appreciated and heard.

There are times that you may have to leave your current job to make the amount of money you want. Yes, change is uncomfortable. But, it may be your only way to make more money. In the event you are in a small town or in an industry where there is nowhere else to work, stay there. Execute your plan for entrepreneurship. The best time to start your business is when you have a job. Your business can generate another stream of income. Meanwhile, your current job can sustain you while you are getting started. Once your business matches or exceeds your job's salary, consider resigning. You can decide to go full time with your business.

2. *"I can never be a millionaire."*
In the book, "Millionaire Next Door", authors Thomas J.

Stanley and William D. Danko point out that there are more millionaires in our lifetime than ever before. Most millionaires average making $130,000 a year. Millionaires tend to live within their means and save a high percentage of their income. If you desire to be a millionaire, work with a professional money manager who can crunch numbers to determine how much money you will need to save now to become a millionaire later.

Thanks to compound interest, invested money multiplies over time. The younger you are when you start investing, the less money you need to invest. For example, if you start saving $50 a week when you are 25 by the time you are 65, you will be a millionaire. If you do not start saving for retirement until you are in your 40s, you have less time for your money to compound. To become a millionaire, you will have to invest more money weekly to become a millionaire by the time you are 65. The lesson here is, the younger you start saving, the more time your money has to grow. The older you start saving, the less time your money has to grow.

It is easier to invest your way to becoming a millionaire than to save a million dollars. A traditional savings account yields less than one percent. A traditional investment account can easily yield an average of 10 percent over the course of 30 years. While this was a crash course on investing, I hope it encourages you to start investing. You can become a millionaire if you want to. Being a millionaire is not as hard as you may think. It requires making decisions today that your future self will thank you for.

3. "If I ever make money, I will lose it."
Joyce Meyer, a Christian author, points out that you have to respect money. Think about money in terms

of how many hours you have to work to make a certain amount. For example, If you make $20 per hour, it takes 10 hours to make $200. If you blow that money in frivolous ways, it's just like setting it afire and watching it go up in flames.

I used to be terrible about blowing my money on dumb things. For example, I paid out $790.00 over the course of five months for red light tickets. I was captured on camera five times with each ticket costing me $158.00. I thought it would get better, but it never did. Then my husband looked at the footage. After viewing the footage, my husband told me that I was at fault each time. I went through three red lights and turned right without yielding on two occasions. It was me. I had the problem. I was going too fast because I was not managing my time well. I had to change. I had to slow down and I had to respect the money I was making. I realized that what I thought was a conspiracy against me, really wasn't.

I was not being a good steward over my time or finances. I was spending $158 per ticket for something I had control over. I do facials as one of my streams of income, and I charge $84 for a one hour customized facial. When I looked at the tickets as a way of giving away 9.5 facials to support my habit of driving irresponsibility and not managing my time, I realized that I had to have a serious conversation with myself about this bad habit.

The underlying factors for making money and losing money are fear, worth and acceptance. Identifying areas in your life that are holding you back requires work. In time, you can overcome and make the amount of money you desire.

4. *"I'm going to end up being like the rest of my family"*

The U.S. Census Bureau reported that nearly 72% of Americans live in or close to the city where they grew up. Knowing this fact can explain why so many people end up like the rest of their family. You assimilate to those you are around. I had to leave Ohio for me to grow. I needed to see something different. I needed to see a change of scenery and see how other people lived and thought. Had I stayed where I was, I would not be where I am now. I had to leave. Being around familiar people creates familiarity. It is hard to grow outside your familiar surroundings. Often, to grow you need to move.

My first three years away from my surroundings were uncomfortable and scary, as I was not always welcomed or embraced. Being in Florida required me to grow up. Because I did not have a lot of friends, I formed an unhealthy relationship with the Publix grocery store. I became friends with their sub sandwiches and chicken wings, and we were together every Friday evening. That was until I went to the doctor to find that I gained 20 pounds since my last visit and had high cholesterol. We eventually broke up.

Once I started discovering me and getting to know different people, I began to assimilate with those around me. I was able to create, dream, imagine and make moves. While I spoke with my family weekly, I did not always tell them my every move. Getting outside of your comfort zone will cause you to grow and think differently.

Leaving your surroundings may be temporary. You may

move to the next town over and those 20 minutes can make a difference in how you see yourself. You may also move to another city, state or country. Leaving your familiar settings creates a paradigm shift in your mind-set. This change in your mindset may offend those who know you. Be careful with what you share because you do not want to offend anyone.They may not understand or like the fact that you have changed. Your change can make others uncomfortable.

Choosing to not be like the rest of your family is up to you. Identify those areas you do not want to repeat and devise a plan. Here are some examples:

1. *"I can never live on my own."*
Living on your own takes time, planning and belief that you can. In many cultures, people live together forever. But, in the United States, people tend to look forward to having their own place. There is a time for you to live on your own and there is a time to live with others.

To live on your own, you need to have good credit and make at least three times more than your rent. If you do not make three times your rent, it will be difficult for you to get approved for an apartment or mortgage. If you are ready to move out on your own but cannot afford it, you may want to consider getting a roommate to split the cost with you.

If you do not have established credit, you may need to get a cosigner for your lease. This is someone who takes on the responsibility of paying your rent in the event you default. This is a lot to ask of someone. If no one agrees to cosign for you, you will need to establish credit on your own. Consider getting a prepaid credit card that will show up on your credit report. Pay an amount upfront and use the money on the card responsibly. Once you do this for a few months and pay the card off, you now have established credit.

If you need to have a roommate, choose one wisely. Make sure the person you select is responsible, pays the bills on time and has good credit. If your chosen roommate does not have a rental history, check three references. Look for character references to ensure this person's lifestyle aligns with yours. If your roommate needs to establish credit, help him or her apply the techniques you recently learned.

Check your motives. Why do you want to live on your own? If you want to live on your own to feel independent and free, then save your money and establish good credit.

If you fear having to move back home, devise a thorough plan and plan for unexpected expenses. Have a saving account of at least $1,000 for emergencies. Consider your monthly utilities before you sign a one-year lease. Whatever you do, live within your means. Grocery shopping and cooking at home instead of eating out daily is a great way to save money.

Living on your own can be a wonderful accomplishment, if you plan for it properly. Take time to make sure that when you move out that you do not have to go back to your original living arrangement.

2. "I will never have enough money to buy a home"

Purchasing a home had been a goal of mine for a very long time. Starting my business was my first goal. Thus, me purchasing a home had to be on the back burner until my business was more established. I had to wait until I was in business for seven years to get a house, and it seemed like forever. But once we finally got our house, I realized the timing was right.

I started preparing for homeownership three years before we got our house. I took several courses on homeownership, spoke to several lenders and worked on my credit. Once we finally purchased our home, the process was easy. There were no major hiccups because we prepared and saved. My realtor commented on how seamless the process was. I believe it was because we planned and prepared for that moment. We were preapproved with a good interest rate because we had good credit. We saved for a down payment and knew what to expect.

Purchasing a home takes time and planning, but it can be achieved. Homeownership is a wonderful accomplishment. You get the opportunity to live the American dream and can decide on what type of home works best for you. There are several home ownership programs available for those who qualify depending on the income bracket you are in.

Just because you qualify for a certain amount of money, doesn't mean that you have to use that entire amount. For example, if you qualify for $300,000 for a mortgage, it does not mean you have to get a $300,000 house. You may realize that to be comfortable with your monthly payment, you need to only spend $225,000. Do not make decisions to impress others but to live within your means.

I always thought that we would live in a new-build, single-family home. When our realtor started driving us around for houses in our price range, I did not like what I saw. I never considered a townhouse until she showed us the one we ended up buying. It was a new-build and felt like a home once we got inside. We selected an end unit so we would have windows and light, as that was an important factor for me. My husband wanted to believe he would mow the lawn, but our previous living situation proved otherwise. We needed a townhouse for our first home purchase based upon our busy lifestyle. Our townhouse was exactly what we needed for our first home purchase.

Set a goal for when you want to buy a home. Begin planning for a house like you already have it and watch how it manifests.

3. *"If they didn't make it, how can I?"*

"They" are not You. A lot of times we perceive other people's stories like they are our experiences. You don't know "their" entire story. You may not know their entire story because it is their story. So, ask some questions and gather information from what you do know about their situation. Figure out ways you can avoid repeating their patterns. Plan to do things differently and watch how things unfold.

I am a firm believer in getting educated and researching before I start something. Some of the best advice I received from one of my educators was to study! She saw that while I thought I was ready to start teaching and accepting students, I wasn't. The time I spent studying prepared me for what was to come. Once the students finally started enrolling, I was ready. I was prepared. I was confident. In turn, I was better able to prepare my students for the industry.

Do not start a business venture until you are ready. Read as many books as you can, study with people in your industry and learn as much as possible. This can save you hundreds and thousands of dollars. Walk in humility and ask questions. Many people do not make it because they started too soon and were not ready, just like I was tempted to do. When I graduated from esthetics school, I had the opportunity to buy a salon and spa. Had I made that move, I would have lost the business because I was not ready or prepared. Many people jump the gun and do things prematurely. They are surprised when things do not work out. Research your industry, study and prepare for the success that is awaiting you.

4. *"I will never have everything I want."*
Write down what you want and be specific about it. What you want, wants you. Something magical happens when you write. It affects you physiologically as you are creating your future. Whether you think you can or think you can't you are correct.

Quit blaming God as an excuse for having less. This is an excuse for laziness, apathy and not going after your dream. God honors the desires of your heart and as long as they are for good and not for evil, you should live out your dream.

Every time I try to get ahead, something happens. So what? Keep pressing and don't throw in the towel too soon. The moment you're ready to quit is usually the moment right before the miracle happens. Keep pressing on and change your perspective when you have temporary setbacks. As long as you are putting one foot in front of the other, you are making progress.

3 | THE DREAM IS NOT JUST FOR YOU

As I reflect back, I ask myself what would have happened if I had not started my business. How would our graduates and present students' lives have been different? Where would my employees be working? Would they be happy? Would I be happy? The fact that I said yes and my willingness to be uncomfortable, affected the lives of others. The flexibility of our online/hybrid program allowed people to make career changes.

BEING UNCOMFORTABLE IS PART OF THE PROCESS

Being uncomfortable is part of the process. During one of our sessions, my coach told me that I have to feel comfortable watching a movie in my own home. To feel comfortable, I had to be in my home. I was trying to follow him, just like you're trying to follow me. I was seeing my business grow faster than my willingness to be uncomfortable. As you are going to the next level, sometimes you will feel displaced. While you are in transition, you are going to feel uncomfortable with the unknown. You will not feel comfortable until you are walking in that next level. After a while, the next level will become comfortable and it will then be your new normal. The very things you feared when pondering your decision will become non-factors. You will become comfortable again, and this represents you watching a movie in your own home.

THE DREAM IS NOT JUST FOR YOU

When you start to live out your dream, you will begin to see that the Dream is not just for you. Here's an example of what I mean:

Think about how long the cellphone has been in existence. If you think it's been since the '80s or even later, you are wrong. If you think it's been around since the '60s, you'd still be wrong. The cell phone has been around ever since the idea existed in the mind of someone. But, it was waiting for the person to manifest it. Who is waiting for your dream to manifest? Who will enjoy it?

People frequently take others to court over the usurpation of intellectual property. But, is it a case of someone stealing an idea or did that person simply manifest it first?

Initially, when starting a business, you may only be thinking about how it will affect you. But, when you tap into how your dream can affect the lives of others, your desires will change. I knew that I wanted to start a business when I moved from Ohio to Florida. I thought I was going to open up a wellness spa with an exercise facility, smoothie bar, salon and spa. For about a year, I tried to write out a business plan for this wellness spa and kept getting stuck when I tried to write out how my business distinguished itself from others.

When I moved to Orlando, I came across a wellness spa that was exactly like what I envisioned. I stopped my car, went inside and asked for a tour of the facility. To the right was a fitness area with treadmills and free weights. There was a door that separated the spa area from the exercise area. I walked through the door and entered the spa. There were four treatment rooms, and each one had a massage table and esthetics equipment. I was impressed with what I saw, but there were no clients or therapists in the treatment rooms. As I walked through the spa, I approached the smoothie bar. No one was working in that area either, but I saw that it was stocked with supplies for smoothies.

I felt like someone stole my idea. The reality is that they manifested what I envisioned. They did not steal my idea; they simply had the same idea and vision and implemented it before I did. I drove past this wellness spa often as a reminder that what I envisioned can be accomplished.

One day I drove past that spa to see that it was no longer in business. My heart sank. I couldn't help but wonder why that idea didn't work. Did the owner run out of money? Had no one enrolled in the gym? Then, a light bulb went off. I reflected on what I saw when I toured the facility. There were only people in the workout area. All the spa rooms were open, but there were no clients or therapists. No one was working in the smoothie shop. There were only people on the treadmill. I do not know the details of why the wellness spa went out of business. Yet, I speculated a bit about their business model.

STREAMLINE YOUR DREAM

Thinking about this business model made me realize that you can have a dream but it needs to be streamlined. Initially, it is difficult to be everything to everyone at once. When pondering about why that spa failed, I thought about my own exercise experiences. Typically, when I'm getting a facial or massage, I don't think about working out. While that idea was great, the fact that there were no clients in the spa area indicated that this part of the business was overlooked. The only place I saw people was in the workout area. Studying this business from afar taught me some important lessons about beginning my own venture. It also changed my focus on starting a wellness spa.

The big vision I had was a school that had several programs like skin care, nail care, massage therapy and advanced skincare classes. But, I was a small business owner occupying a small space with limited resources. There was no way I could start my business with all these programs. Since I only had a small space to work in, I needed to put a spin on what I had and specialize in it. I chose to specialize in skin care and use words such as "boutique-style" and "specialty program" to capitalize on the fact that my school was so small. I wanted prospective students to feel embraced by a warm and inviting setting. I wanted them to feel like they were at home, and that is exactly what prospective students said they felt upon their arrival.

FOCUS ON WHAT YOU HAVE

Entrepreneurs are visionaries. We see the big picture. Often, we want to start BIG. Instead, take a different tack. Rather than focusing on what you don't have, focus on what you do have. What is in your hands? I can guarantee you that if you have a dream deep inside, you will eventually get everything you need. You may not have everything you want now, but it will come.

Focus on what you have on hand. For example, if you make great cookies, you may not have a shop, but you do have flour. Bake as many cookies as possible. Put cookies in your child's lunch box to take to school to share with other kids. Cover the cookies in plastic wrap and include a label with your contact information and a message that you're accepting orders. Get a separate phone line and dedicated email address to keep your business contacts separate from your personal ones.

Focus on the "Yes"es you get instead of the "No"s. In business, people will frequently turn down whatever it is you are offering. This is not them saying "No" to you, but to your product or business. Do not take it personally. Move on to the next lead or prospect. While some people may not believe in your vision and dream, others will. That's just part of the process. Focus on those who want what you are offering instead of those who do not.

Develop your Niche. Apple is the perfect example of a company that developed their niche well. Formerly, they were Apple Computers. Steve Jobs decided that he did not want the company to be limited to building computers. So, he removed the word "computer" from the name, and they became Apple. The name "Apple" carries with it the idea of quality consumer electronics. Although some people may argue that they are overpriced, Apple focused more on being a specialty than a commodity. Apple distinguished itself from the rest. Since the word "computer" is not associated with Apple, it is not limited to computers. Apple can come out with an iChair, iTable, iCloth. No matter what they create, people will associate it with high quality.

Determine what makes you stand out. Know what makes you different and distinguished. There is a specific audience for you because what you want, wants you. The more specialized you are, the quicker you will attract your targeted audience. For example, the mom who makes cookies can focus on the fact that her cookies are gluten-free and made with coconut oil. Making delicious cookies within these parameters can become her niche.

You cannot be everything to everyone. If you are a people-pleaser, you are going to have to develop thick skin as an entrepreneur and dream builder. If someone calls my school and asks if we offer financial aid, we say up front that we don't. We then have to overcome this obstacle by explaining that while we don't have financial aid, we offer affordable extended payment plans options. We do not discuss these options over the phone because we want the student to tour our specialized campus first. There are times that this statement does not suffice and it is quickly followed by a dial tone. It makes you wonder if the person cared more about the opportunity to receive financial aid or attending a quality, specialized program. The person who hung up has already predetermined that without financial aid attending our program is impossible, when in reality, this may not be the case.

Our targeted audience focuses on a few details. They want to find a specialized program that offers quality skincare training. They have time constraints and like the idea of having an online/hybrid option. Our audience knows that skincare is what they want to do and is focused on specializing in this area. They also like the fact that we offer small class sizes that allow them to receive individualized attention. We focus on these key points when we do our tours. What we want, wants us. If both parties are in agreement that what we offer is what they are looking for, we proceed. The prospective student enrolls. It's that simple. We do not focus on money. It's amazing to see how many people figure out the financing. It becomes easier when they realize they have found the program suitable for them.

KNOW YOUR WORTH AND BE COMFORTABLE ASKING FOR IT

Do not charge someone a price you are uncomfortable asking for. Know your worth, but be comfortable with the amount you are charging. I have never subscribed to discounting my prices. My prices are what they are because of my education, quality of the products and my expertise. So, I have no reason to discount my prices. It makes no sense to me to do so. I did run Groupon promotions a few times when I first started my business. This tactic can help you get started with search engine optimization (SEO) and get your name out there. But, advertising on Groupon did not yield me loyal clients. I received rave reviews from clients who came to me and said they would return, but ultimately they never did. If someone only pays $50 for a facial through Groupon, it is likely hard for them to pay more. They will not want to pay my regular, non-discounted prices for my services. My experience has been that they look for a $50 Groupon for the same services from somewhere else. I now have a very select, by-referral-only, targeted client base. I charge what I charge and I do not discount my prices. I will offer a free add-on, but will not discount my prices. My clients value me, my expertise and enjoy my services.

I once worked with a spa owner who offered massages and facials. One day, I helped her with a few facials. At the end of the treatment, I watched her cash out her clients. She told her clients that the cost of the service was $260 but that she would take off 20 percent.

I looked at her perplexed. After the clients left, I asked her why she discounted her prices. She said that she felt bad asking them for so much money. I gasped and asked why she didn't just change her prices to what she was comfortable with. Discounting your prices is nothing more than training your client on how to treat you. You are essentially saying, "I am not worth $260".

DEVELOPING AN ELEVATOR PITCH FOR YOUR TARGET AUDIENCE

Identify who your target audience is for your dream to become a reality. Take some time to figure it out. Who is your dream for? When you think of your dream, think about who is benefitting from it. Knowing these answers will help you develop your 10-second elevator pitch that includes an explanation of who you are, what you do and how someone can benefit from your business. For example, my elevator pitch is: Elise Esthetics Institute is the first online/hybrid skincare program in the state of Florida. We specialize in skincare. You can receive your facial specialist license in as few as five months. This pitch summarizes who we are, what we do and how someone can benefit from our program.

Be concise in explaining what you do and who you are. Droning on and on endlessly will annoy many people. So, keep it short and sweet. The average attention span is roughly 20 seconds. So, if you've gone on beyond that amount of time, everything you said goes unnoticed. When you are direct and concise in explaining what you do, who it's for and how they can benefit, people will be drawn to you. Give them just enough to ask for more. If someone is interested, they will ask questions.

THE CLASSY HUSTLE

Once, I had a brunch meeting with some other businesswomen. We spent the time taking turns explaining how we implemented our 10-second elevator pitch. One of the ladies started her pitch explaining four different businesses she has. After she was finished, I encouraged her to focus on one business venture at a time. I told her to consider the function she's attending, who her audience is and which business she wants to focus on. Since she has four businesses, she needs to develop four separate, 10-second elevator speeches and only mention one business when she introduces herself. That way she could avoid mentioning all four businesses and coming across as being a "jack-of-all-trades-and-master-of none".

You are the original manuscript. There is no one like you and no one with your handprints. What's for you is for you. It does not matter if anyone else has a similar idea. Other people's ideas are not yours. They are not YOU. Once you tap into what makes you unique and special, some beautiful things will begin to unfold. You will realize that YOU are what makes your dream unique. Be careful with whom you share your dreams, as they may be people whose primary goal is to block your dream. Surround yourself with people who will encourage you to dream bigger! Use past experiences, hurts, frustrations and pains to propel you forward. My dad calls this "forward frustration". As long as you are moving forward, you are making progress. Determine what your dream is and who it is for. Know your worth and spend time focusing on what is in your hand.

4 | WHILE YOU WAIT

Waiting is difficult for several reasons. We are born impatient and we want what we want, when we want it. Think about a brand new baby who is hungry. The baby gets hungry and screams until you satisfy the hunger. Waiting for a business to manifest can test your patience and can be challenging, as it is just like giving birth to a child.

YOUR DREAM IS JUST LIKE YOUR BABY

You carry your dream just like it's a baby. If you try to give birth to your dream too soon, you will miscarry it. Miscarrying a vision or dream is failing to attain the desired end or to be unsuccessful in attaining the intended purpose. Having experienced miscarriages of babies, I realize that there was a reason my body rejected the pregnancies. My body knew that there would be problems if I carried the fetuses to full-term. The physiological purpose of pregnancy is to allow the fetus to develop into a healthy baby. Something was not right, something was not developed, therefore, my body rejected the pregnancy. I know in time that we will have a healthy child, whether through natural means or through adoption. When I am ready, a child will come.

PUTTING TOGETHER YOUR BAIL TEAM

The Hebrew word for wait, "Qavah", means to expect, hope or look for with eager expectation. That is the exact attitude you need while you are waiting for your dream to come to fruition. While you are waiting for your business to manifest, you must prepare for success. While I was waiting for approval to open my school, I took classes from the Small Business Development Center. After I successfully completed the program, I received a certificate of completion, which I was able to use to apply for a small business loan. Although my circumstances did not qualify me to get a loan, these classes prepared me for business ownership, as they let me know exactly who I needed on my team. I like to call this team the "BAIL team."

Establish your BAIL team while you are waiting for your dream to manifest. There will be no need for a BAIL out when you have relationships established with these four trusted people:

B - Banker.

The topic of money makes a lot of people uncomfortable. How you grow up can determine your outlook on money. I grew up very materialistic, viewing money as a tool to get things. I never understood the purpose of money or how to make it grow. My goal in life and in working in corporate America was to always make more money. I never questioned my reasoning for wanting more, as I assumed this was a desire for most people.

Along my entrepreneurial journey, I realized that I wanted freedom more than money. Up until this time, I never sat down to analyze what mattered to me. I thought I had to make a certain amount of money to live and to be happy.

Being an entrepreneur fueled me in a way I never imagined. It gave me the ammunition I needed to survive. It was a feast or famine situation. You don't know what you are made of until you have eliminated all your comforts. While depending on yourself is scary, there is an excitement that follows it.

Most bankers at local branches are in the same rat race as the consumers they serve. At first, I didn't see the need to establish a relationship with a banker unless I needed an "NSF" fee reversed. Then, I met a banker who understood and respected the heart of an entrepreneur. He gave me a strategy, wisdom and the tools I needed to look attractive to lenders.

Currently, I have relationships with four bankers who are all in upper-level management. I have their personal cell phone numbers and have been granted the permission to contact them when I need to. Two of the four bankers have been responsible for granting me lines of credit. The third banker has approved me for a commercial loan for over one million dollars.

I maintained a relationship with only one bank for many years. After those years, I realized that I needed to have several bankers whom I could call on. I grew amazed at how many bankers wanted to see me and my business succeed. Once the banks saw my successful track record of growing my business and wealth, they were willing to lend me money. My advisors suggested that I remain debt-free until I was ready to take on strategic debt by way of a commercial loan.

A - Accountant.
Hire a reputable accountant who knows the specific laws for your industry. I made the mistake of hiring several reputable accountants who did not know how to do accounting for schools. There is a specific way

the Department of Education expects schools to report finances. When I would go to Commission meetings, I would get in trouble for reporting inaccurately. I was finally given a list of referrals for accounting firms that specialized in accounting for schools.

I started making phone calls to the companies on the list. After making several phone calls, I was finally able to speak to an accountant. Instead of berating me for my ignorance and negligence, I received a warm response. She was understanding and kind. She understood my plight and was more than willing to help me get my business back on track. I was concerned about the cost of hiring an accounting firm. The idea of having an accounting firm sounded so grand. She reassured me that she would work with me. Over the course of our seven-year relationship, she has worked with me and has given me lots of wise advice.

She was adamant about me learning how to do my own bookkeeping. For years, I hated doing my books. But, through this practice, I was able to understand my business better. After four years of doing my own bookkeeping, I was finally able to hire a professional bookkeeping firm. I was able to understand the details of what they were doing because of my previous experience of doing it myself. When you have a reputable accounting firm managing your finances, you can rest easy at night. You won't have to worry about Uncle Sam confiscating any cars or houses.

I - Insurance Agent.

You must have insurance to protect yourself, your assets and your business. You can choose from a number of different types of policies for your business. Hire an insurance agent who is reputable and honest and who will help you find the best rates possible. Although having an insurance policy may appear to be an unnecessary expense, failing to have insurance can result in serious repercussions. Be sure to have the right amount of coverage. There is a fine line between not having enough insurance and being over-insured. Make sure that you know and understand the difference.

L - Lawyer.

Seeking legal counsel is crucial when determining how to set up your business. Receiving this counsel can save you years of heartache and headaches. I encourage you to research or seek references for a good business attorney. Set up an appointment with a lawyer before making large investments so you can protect yourself and your assets. You may find that it is not necessary to keep an attorney on retainer. But, spending a small amount of money upfront can save you time and money in the long run. I am still surprised by how many business owners are operating as a sole proprietorship. They are operating as a business with limited protection. It may take some time to set up your business with the right classification. Taking the time to consult with an attorney can help you get the right tax savings. Once your business gets more established, consider having an attorney on retainer.

PRINCIPLES I LIVE BY

Even with establishing my "BAIL" team, there are certain principles I choose to live by. This is where faith comes in. The principles I live by are, simply put: Where God Guides, He Provides and Timing Does not Matter as Much as Trusting the Process.

WHERE GOD GUIDES, HE PROVIDES

I first heard "Where God guides, He provides" from a pastor at my church. I chose to hold on to these words for dear life when I started my business. I had extremely limited resources and quickly ran out of money. The one fact about starting a business with no money is that it takes an element of faith. I say "an element of faith" instead of a "lot of faith." Because the Bible states that faith the size of a mustard seed is all that is needed. Starting a business requires faith. Faith is believing what you can't see in the physical sense.

TIMING DOESN'T MATTER AS MUCH AS TRUSTING THE PROCESS

The second principle, "Timing doesn't matter as much as trusting the process" is proven by the fact that it took about four months of waiting for me to get approval for the school. Looking back, four months does not seem like a long time. But, during the process, four months seemed like an eternity. The Department of Education did not allow me to start marketing the school until it was approved. As soon as the school received its approval in September 2011, I hit the ground running. I began to share the news about the school using the limited marketing resources I had available. I had to start recruiting students to survive.

My goal was to start my first class in January, 2012. I had written down all my goals in my business plan, including the start date. As I interviewed prospective students, I shared my vision for the school. I used the fact that they would be the "first" class as a selling point. I was excited about the fact that I had enrolled three students to start classes in January.

During the weeks leading up to the start of the first class, I received phone calls from all of my students cancelling their enrollment. They all stated that they were unable to start due to mitigating circumstances. I was distraught, hurt, frustrated and felt defeated. What was I to do now? How was I going to live? How was I going to pay my rent? How was I going to make it?

The following month was a blur. I was feeling so vulnerable I wanted to just lay on the floor in my living/work suite the entire month in a fetal position. I felt a sense of safety going back to a childlike state with childlike beliefs.

In my most vulnerable moments, I felt a sense of safety on that floor. I knew that when I got up, everything was going to be ok. After my temper tantrum, I went back to recruiting. I beat the pavement with marketing and told everyone I knew about my school.

While I was waiting, I had to get a part time job through a temporary agency. I needed to work to pay bills but did not want a long-term commitment with a company. I worked several front desk positions while I actively recruited at night and on my days off. I was always offered jobs by the company I worked for, and I was always tempted to go back to the security of corporate America. I struggled with the idea of working a 9-to-5 job rather than work for myself. I wondered if I could actually sustain myself.

While I waited, opportunities began to present themselves. I decided to start doing facials and using my space to open a spa. Within months I had two businesses: a school and a spa. I began marketing my spa services and building a client base.

THE CLASSY HUSTLE

The school was my main focus, and I needed to collaborate with a skincare line. I met with one business consultant to learn more about her skincare line. I decided that I would go with this product line but did not have the money to open up the account. During our meeting, I was honest about that fact.

A few months after our meeting, the skincare company asked me about subleasing my living/work space. But, first they wanted to confirm that it was my intention to use their line once I got the money. I told them that was my intention. They needed a place to hold their classes while they were setting up their new location and wanted to know if they could sublease my living/working space for a few months. They asked how much I would charge for rent. I was ecstatic about the idea of not having to worry about the rent for a period of time. This was exactly the opportunity I needed.

I had the opportunity to be an intern in my own school. I was able to come into my space and learn from some of the best educators in the skincare industry. I was being trained for free while having my rent paid. I did have to move out for a few months and stayed with a friend. I could not afford to be "found out" about my living arrangement, and the company needed full access to my space.

The company came in and showed me how to run my school. They brought in all their equipment and set up my space to look like a learning institution. I watched in amazement as they arranged things according to their specifications.

After attending their classes for several months, I was ready. **I was ready to birth my vision.** I finally received the phone call I dreamed of. A prospective student's mother called about her daughter's interest in my school. The daughter had seen our school on Yelp. I was about the 12th page on the Google search. Her mother started asking questions about the school. I answered each question to the best of my ability. The mom asked when the next class started. At this point, I had given up scheduling start dates. So instead of answering, I asked when her daughter wanted to start. In the background, I heard her daughter respond that she wanted to start as soon as possible.

I put the phone on speaker to check an available date on the calendar and gave her the date of Monday, September 17". That was in 2012. The mom, her daughter and I scheduled a time to meet. Once we met, the prospective student indicated that she had a friend who wanted to enroll as well. The mom and her daughter asked how many other students would be joining them. At that point, I told them that the two girls are the only enrollees so far. Those two young ladies were the first two students at my school.

I realized that timing didn't matter as much as my preparation. When I was ready, the students came. Had I started in January, when I thought I was ready, my school would have miscarried. The timing of when the first class started was perfectly perfect.

5 | DO NOT COMPARE YOURSELF TO OTHERS

There's an expression that says comparison kills. Do you believe this statement? Does comparison really kill? I would argue that even if you do not literally die, your dream and uniqueness do. When you compare yourself to someone else, you diminish your worth and uniqueness. Focusing your attention on someone else takes away from what's inside you.

While I was starting my school, I did not look at other schools' websites for ideas. I knew that if I did that it would hinder my creativity and I would end up assimilating to what they created. I knew that what was for me was for me. I also knew that when someone went to my website, it needed to reflect me and my vision for the school. There is no school that is exactly like mine, not even close, because the owners of other schools are not me. The same goes for you, too. Comparing your idea to someone else's diminishes your own ideas.

When I would meet with prospective students, I loved hearing them tell me that my school came across just as it did on my website. I used the same person to photograph my school and create my website, and this decision paid off. His look and feel is consistent with what I wanted to create. He was able to design my website based on what he knew about me and my vision. Because he knew me, he was able to graphically capture what I wanted to present. While I was unable to create it, I was able to tell him what I envisioned. Make sure that the person you hire to create your graphics, website and logo knows and understands both you and your vision. You need to invest in what you want to create. Your online presence should encapsulate your uniqueness and vision for your business.

WHAT'S WRONG WITH ME?

In my quest for figuring out why I was so different growing up, I discovered a few things. I began to understand more about my uniqueness after embracing being an entrepreneur. I realized that entrepreneurship was in my blood. Once this reality embodied me, I felt accepted for the first time ever.

I never really fit in, even as a child. I was always a bit of a misfit. This fact reality set in on my first trip to Washington, D.C. as a Girl Scout, during my preteen years. I thought I had two best friends. That was until the girls went around the bus naming who their best friends were. Once it got to me, I could no longer answer because the two people I thought were my best friends did not mention my name. I was so embarrassed and did not want to cause more embarrassment and shame to myself, so I chose to be quiet. But, my heart ached at the reality of not having a best friend. To this day, I will not refer to someone as being my best friend for fear of the feeling not being reciprocated. I digress. I would call my husband my best friend.

For years, this memory reality haunted me, and I wanted to know why I was no one else's best friend. What was it about me?

The first paper I wrote when I was in college addressed

this reality. I was always insecure with my writing, so I was thrilled when I received a B- on this paper. The professor was very complimentary with my attempt to write a good paper. She felt the pain that I was trying to express and could relate. I chose to ignore the pain that plagued me and focused on my grade of a B-.

One of the reasons the B- grade was so meaningful was because of my struggle to write. I had to ask my oldest sister to help me write what I was trying to say. I struggled with putting words on paper. I had writers block all the time. So the fact that I am writing this book is a miracle and gives me a sense of accomplishment.

While I am still indecisive about the need to have a "best friend", I have chosen not to care too much. I prefer to focus on who is rooting for me rather than focusing on who does not want to be my friend. I am very selective on who I give my energy to. Everyone is not deserving of me. While that is a bold statement, I know who I am and what I possess. Anyone connected to me will become a better person because I am choosing to be a better person. I also realize that the people I previously wanted to be "best friends" with are now just my Facebook friends, and I am content with not having them in my inner circle.

DARE TO BE DIFFERENT

You have to be content with being alone. Dare to be different. As I reflect back, even at a young age, I was very different. I dared to ask pensive questions, even at the expense of offending others. I was on a quest for knowledge and I wanted to know "the whys" behind things. Even today, when I coach, train and teach others, I always find myself answering "the whys."

I had a strict upbringing in a Pentecostal church, the other people in the church did not always embrace my uniqueness. The church people were not always accepting of a child asking so many questions. When I was 12 years old, I walked up to the microphone and asked a question at a church meeting called "The Saint's Meeting". I asked why we weren't allowed to go to the movies. This question had been bothering me for a while. When our pastor answered that the movies were not designed for the saints or church people, I was perplexed. I further asked, why then were we allowed to go to the mall, as I did not think the mall was designed for church people or saints either. The questions I stirred up caused me to have a reputation for being challenging. Looking back, I can understand why.

Based upon my childhood experiences of not fitting in, I resorted to fantasizing. It was a way I escaped. In college, I became concerned about how much time I was spending fantasizing. So much so, that I confided in one of my college professors that I thought I had a learning disability. He looked at me sideways trying to figure out how I completed four years of college with passing grades. He did not understand how I completed four year of business school while having a learning disability. My average GPA was around a 2.7 because I didn't concentrate on studying much. He told me to go to the learning center to take a test to find out how I learned.

I took the VAK Learning Styles test. I learned that there are three ways we learn: visual, auditory and kinesthetic. The test indicated that I was a visual learner. Most of the lectures I had to sit through in the '90s were completely auditory and, therefore, boring to me. The way I dealt with boredom was fantasizing about life after class and what I would do after college. I also discovered that I was on the dyslexia spectrum.

The professor encouraged me to embrace how I learned. He told me to go to each of my professors and tell them about my test results. Instead of lecturing, he told me to ask them to provide visual tools to help to keep my attention. Surprisingly, the professors concurred, as they were open to helping me succeed. Each of them started incorporating PowerPoint presentations in their lectures. It resulted in me making the Dean's List for the first time ever. I was actually excelling in class!

Now, I am outgoing and an extravert by nature. I also embrace having quiet time while challenging my thoughts. I like to know what I am thinking about and why I am thinking the way I am. I categorize my thoughts in two ways. My thoughts are either empowering or disempowering. Empowering thoughts are positive and uplifting thoughts. Disempowering thoughts are those with negative outcomes that are self-serving. I constantly challenge my thinking. No one but you knows what you are thinking, so it can be easy to hide your thoughts. Proverbs 23:7 states, "As a man thinketh in his heart, so is he". My thoughts affect my words and my words affect my outcome. I chose to think empowering thoughts and say words that speak life!

It is important to not compare yourself to others because entrepreneurs think differently. Not everyone has the intestinal fortitude to be an entrepreneur. Here are some of the characteristics it takes to be an entrepreneur:

Being Different

When you watch a movie that features a success story, the entrepreneurs are typically different. Even in childhood, they went against the status quo. They went against the norm. They thought outside the box and were often made fun of. That was the story of my life. I was different and was not afraid to challenge the status quo. I pondered what people said. I was curious about why people uttered certain words. People intrigued me, which prompted me to ask a lot of questions. For example, when I was a child, I asked a single mother at my church where her husband was. She must have said that she divorced. Of course, I followed that up by asking why. She told my mom about my behavior, and it became obvious that I stepped on her toes and that she did not like me. My mom told me that there are just some things we cannot say, that being one of them. I understood what she was trying to say, but years later I am still challenged in this area.

The adolescent years of future entrepreneurs may be difficult for their parents. The parents need to understand the mindset of a future-entrepreneur child. Their disinterest in what's "normal" may be a sign of their entrepreneurial spirit. They defy all odds. They may appear to be combative. They ask a lot of questions.

As a parent, it is important for you to tap into your children's interests. Then, you will need to tap into cultivating their gifts instead of squelching them.

It is amazing how many people I encounter who share their unfulfilled dreams with me. After probing to learn more, I usually discover that it was those closest to them who killed their dreams. Being misunderstood is a dangerous thing. It is even more dangerous when that person has the power to alter your course in life.

Struggles are Necessary for Success

During the initial stages of starting my business, I struggled. There were times I did not know how I was going to pay my rent. One day, I received a phone call from a close friend. She inquired about how my business was going. I admitted that it was tough and I didn't know how I was going to pay my rent the upcoming month. She responded with great pity. She told me that she was going to see what she and her husband could do to help me. After a while, she sent me an encouragement card with $300.00. I was grateful. I was also even more motivated!

Their gift made me realize that I needed to stay the course of entrepreneurship, especially if I planned on achieving financial freedom. I appreciated their monetary help and used it to pay part of my rent. Their gift helped me to realize that working in corporate America would always present limitations on how much money you can make. This realization motivated me to keep going even though I was uncomfortable.

A few years later, my husband and I were at my friend's birthday party and mingling with some of her friends. We met a couple whose daughter was contemplating going to esthetics school. The parents were at a crossroads. They wanted to support their daughter but did not want her to leave a four-year college to pursue a career in makeup. My husband told the gentleman about my career in esthetics as well as my school. He shared with the father how I had become successful as a makeup artist and esthetician. The father was so appreciative for my husband sharing my success. He felt like he and his wife received the confirmation they needed to support their daughter.

The girl's father told my friend's husband about his excitement. He shared that he could now support his daughter's decision. Instead of focusing on this good news, my friend's husband told him about the struggles I had starting up my school. It was hard for him to acknowledge my successes.

I decided that the best way to thank my friend and her husband for their gift was to send them the money they had given me. My friend was shocked about me sending them a check because the money had been given as a gift. I knew that it was, but I wanted to make sure that the next time the story was told about the start-up for my business that my successes trumped my struggles. My struggles were necessary and resulted in my ability to pay back what was given to me.

I began to realize after associating with several entrepreneurs that we all had some aspects in common. We are tenacious, risk-takers, multitaskers and courageous!

Being Tenacious (Having a Pitbull Mindset)
One day early in our marriage, my husband and I were having a meaningful conversation — until he said that I was a pitbull. The look I gave him following that statement was intense. I thought that he was trying to nicely call me the "B word". I began to interrogate him, asking him what he meant. He tried to explain, but the more he explained, the more offended I became. We decided to end the conversation once we saw the conversation escalating, but going nowhere. A few months followed, and my husband called me a pitbull again. But this time, it was because of something I did.

One day I had the opportunity to ask one of his friends some questions about his dating life. It was obvious that the gentleman was uncomfortable with my questions, and instead of saying that, he tried to avoid answering my questions. The more he avoided answering me, the more I interrogated him. Eventually, he answered my questions, and my husband, who had witnessed the entire scene, responded that my actions in that situation were a prime example of why he called me a pitbull. His comment immediately prompted me to study the pitbull breed more.

That's when I was finally able to hear what my husband had been trying to say. I was relentless. I did not give up. I will not stop at a "no". He was equating my mindset to the characteristics of a pitbull. Pitbulls will fight until their death, and they do not give up. I finally realized that my husband had been trying to give me a compliment in a weird type of way. He was telling me that I was tenacious.

Besides the pitbull being relentless, they are one of the most loving, feared and misunderstood breeds. Pitbulls are strong, energetic, agile and powerful dogs. They are also compassionate, protective, resourceful and driven. They are known for their determination and put their heart and soul into whatever they do. I chose to have a pitbull mindset!

Taking Risks and Planning Effectively

Entrepreneurs must be willing to take risks. Every choice has a risk associated with it, and it doesn't always feel good. But, you can balance risk with effective planning, this is referred to as calculated risk. They should balance each other out. I once had a student who worked for Ulta for about eight months. She was a shy introvert at first. But, when she started getting clients to receive facial services, her confidence began to soar and she thought she was ready to open her own skincare business. Her husband was willing to invest in her business, and they started purchasing equipment. They rented a small suite that cost $400 a month to rent. They both thought the price was affordable. She started her business with one client, who she took from Ulta. He received services about once every six weeks. She paid her rent from her household expenses because she did not have enough clients to sustain her business.

After about six months, she closed her business. She reached out to me to ask if I wanted to purchase some of her equipment, which I gladly did for 50 percent of what she paid for it. While she took a risk, it was not a calculated one. There is no way having one client can sustain your business, no matter how affordable the rent is. She needed at least 20 established clients to be able to afford her rent and to pay herself. In reality, she was paying the business to be in business. After she closed the business, she told me that she wished she would have listened to my advice of building her clientele while she worked at Ulta. But, she thought otherwise and paid the price.

My desire is that everyone who wants to be in business for themselves has their own business. But, to be successful, you need to be ready for it. Just because you are frustrated with working for someone else, doesn't mean it is time to start your business. Start planning one-to-two years before you go into business. Crunch numbers to figure out how many clients or customers you will need to cover your overhead and to pay yourself. Consider your savings. If you do not have money saved, you need to start ASAP.

You may have to downsize your living expenses while you start your business. Try getting a roommate or moving in with family and paying off your credit card debt to save on expenses. Do what you have to do to start your business, and understand that the first five years will be the hardest. Stop unnecessary spending, figure out the bare minimum you can live on and learn how to be frugal.

When I first started my business, I had to work part-time for the first four years. I did not receive a paycheck from my business until the third year. For the first three years, the money the business made went back into the business. Since I occupied the same space with my business, my personal expenses were cut in half. I had to put my student loans on hold until I could afford to start paying them again. I kept my living expenses to a minimum. I sacrificed so that I could pay all the expenses for my business.

While I am not an expert on this subject, I do have some opinions on why some businesses fail. Risk-taking is often not the problem for the entrepreneur. Instead, it is a failure to plan effectively.

If you hate taking risks, it doesn't mean you are not cut out to be an entrepreneur. It just means you need to feel comfortable because you value safety and security. So, you may have to have someone push you off the cliff once you have effectively planned. In reality, beginning may be difficult for some people. Focus on your strengths so that your business will be long-lasting and self-sustaining.

What I Gained From My Learning Disorder
A few years ago, I met a client in our student spa who

was a speech pathologist. Her specialty was in helping children who suffered from dyslexia. I was immediately drawn to her since I had been diagnosed with a mild form of dyslexia as an adult. For me, it comes out when I'm extremely tired. I say words backwards and it takes a lot of effort for me to give instructions. It can also be difficult to explain right from left. I have found it very helpful to put up the letter L, using my left hand to process right from left. While I can talk about it very matter of factly now, having this disability caused me to carry some shame. I was embarrassed by it. Having a sense of humor helped me to camouflage this disability.

After talking to this speech pathologist, she reassured me that I was special and unique. She said dyslexic people make some of the best entrepreneurs! I was blown away by what she said. While I can't answer why, I can confirm that becoming an entrepreneur made me feel like I fit in for the first time in my life. It is reassuring knowing that those with disabilities can have successful careers.

Being Courageous
Expect to be criticized and misunderstood when you are an entrepreneur. Most likely, you have been a little odd for most of your life. It takes courage to live out your dream! Not everyone will believe in your vision. I was amazed at next-level relationships that formed from starting my business. While you can expect criticism, you can also expect strangers to encourage you. I learned this lesson when I least expected it.

I learned some valuable lessons by reaching out to other business owners. Their words of encouragement were exactly what I needed. They were like depths of living water that quenched my thirst. Some of the business owners in my neighborhood breathed life into me while I was in the fetal position, not knowing what to do. I was complaining to a nail salon owner about not getting any financing. He challenged me about my belief system. I believed that I needed a loan to sustain my business. In reality, I did not. He told me to eat slowly and I will get full. His words of wisdom resonated into my entire being. I felt a sense of calm and was able to slow down my thoughts.

The pace I was trying to go would not be able to sustain my business in the long run. I needed to slow down and enjoy the journey. There were lots of lessons I needed to learn.

I went through the Small Business Administration's Entrepreneurship course. In my business planning class, the instructor of the program challenged my tuition cost. She asked the other students in the class which one of them would pay my set price for tuition. I was taken aback by her statement and wanted to challenge her belief. So, I stayed after class to address her concerns. I followed her through the building as she turned the lights off so I could get an answer. The pitbull was in full operation. She said that she did not believe that a working adult would have the funds to finance my tuition. I disagreed and refused to budge on my projected tuition cost.

I decided to invite her to be a guest at the graduation ceremony for my second class of students. She drove in the rain to attend. I welcomed her openly and thanked her for attending. I invited her to meet the students who paid for their education. She told me that she was wrong and that I saw something she didn't see. It takes courage to believe what others can't see.

I began to have unwavering faith. My faith was that who I was looking for, was looking for me. Eventually we were able to finally meet each other.

6 | KEEP YOUR WORD

I woke up one Monday morning fatigued and irritated because I hadn't been able to say no to an invitation to a birthday party. In saying yes to the invitation, I chose to honor someone else instead of the commitment I made to myself to keep Sunday as my day of rest and relaxation, as this is the only day I do not work. For the rest of that week, I paid for my decision. My week was a blur and my thoughts were clouded. It was hard for me to get it together until it dawned on me that I had not rested. There are times that you have to say no to invitations so that you can rest.

SAY WHAT YOU MEAN AND MEAN WHAT YOU SAY

Keeping your word is a quality that will distinguish you as a business owner. It speaks of your character and causes people to respect you. We live in a society where we are often surprised when people follow through on their promises. If there is someone I am interested in getting to know, I follow up with action. If I'm asked to go to lunch, I check my calendar and set up a time right away. Many people are shocked at my actions and consider me to be a planner. In reality, I am prioritizing that relationship and implementing honoring my word.

Say what you mean and mean what you say. This statement summarizes the importance of keeping your word. Stand firm with certainty on the decisions you make. There is an old saying that goes, "Even if you are wrong, Be Strong and Wrong." You need to trust yourself. Not every commitment is worth making but every commitment made is worth keeping.

As I was growing up, when my mom got frustrated she would always say that she said what she meant and meant what she said. Her words usually followed with some form of discipline, which led to me crying and being frustrated, all because I did not heed to her warning.

In business, you can't physically assault others for their behavior. But, what you can do is follow through with your words. So, be sure to say what you mean and be prepared to take action. When I taught, I had to write down a lot of things I said because otherwise I would forget because I had too much on my mind. I started writing things down and delegating someone to hold me accountable. When my students saw me following through, they took what I said seriously.

Margaret Paul, the best selling author of "Inner Bonding" says there are two possible reasons why people do not keep their word. The first reason is because they want to control how someone else feels about them. The other possibility is that someone says "yes" with the intent of following through, but ultimately that person does not want to feel controlled and go into resistance mode. It is more important to that person to not be controlled than in keeping his or her word.

I once witnessed an interaction between a mom and her child that was very insightful. The mom and I were talking about New Orleans while her daughter was standing next to us listening to the conversation. She told her daughter that she was going to take her to New Orleans in the summer. Her daughter mumbled a comment that indicated that she thought her mother was lying. A few months later, I followed up with the mom and found out that she, in fact, did not take her daughter to New Orleans. There must have been a reason why the daughter knew that her mom would not follow through with the promise. My guess is that it had likely happened before and the daughter knew that her mother's promises were not sincere.

Your character speaks of who you are and is reflected in what you do. So, by keeping your word, you are framing your character. The more I deal with successful people, the quicker our meetings get. My coaches schedule a 30-minute weekly conference call. Within that timeframe we can have a meaningful and effective conversation. Once you cut to the chase, you can hone in on key points. In most instances, my coaches give me instructions, I agree to do what they suggest and the meeting concludes.

BUILDING AUTHENTIC RELATIONSHIPS

An important factor of being able to keep your word is to be selective in what you commit to. By overcommitting, you stretch yourself out too thin. When I first started my business, I was told to "Network, network, network." Many people believe this is the key to building your business. I attended several networking events. After a few months of attending, I experienced burnout and could not figure out why. Then it hit me, the other people at the events I attended wanted something from me. I also wanted something from them. When both people are taking, no one is giving. This system was not effective and was not yielding results.

I chose to change my approach. I used my time wisely and found common ground with people to see how I could help their business grow. Once my mindset changed from getting something to giving something, I was able to form meaningful and authentic relationships. This practice is now being referred to as netweaving instead of networking.

Authentic relationship building is something I knew I could commit to. I started being intentional with setting lunch dates and getting to know people. I wanted to understand their business needs. Whenever I attended any social or networking event, I would pay attention to who I connected with. If a person drained me after talking to them for a few minutes, I would put that person into the "no" category. If I had something in common with a colleague, that person would go into the "maybe" or "yes" category. If I immediately felt a connection, I would schedule a lunch date. This process helped me maximize my time while preserving my energy.

In deciding which events you will attend, consider if the events are purposeful, intentional and strategic. If you are unable to check each box, consider staying home and maximizing your time in other ways.

INTROVERTS CAN BE ENTREPRENEURS

Many people have stereotypes about entrepreneurs. Many people think that an entrepreneur must have an outgoing personality, be a go-getter, have charisma and be outspoken. The entrepreneur is thought to have a take-charge personality. Because of this stereotype, soft spoken, anti-social, reserved people often think they cannot be entrepreneurs. This couldn't be further from the truth. Some of the most successful entrepreneurs in the world are introverts. Mark Zuckerberg, Bill Gates and Warren Buffet are some examples.

Introverts can make some of the best entrepreneurs. At first, you may be uncomfortable in entrepreneurial endeavors such as networking, public speaking, and leadership roles but with minor adjustment, these endeavors can become your strengths. When you understand your personality type, you will know how to plan. Instead of attending networking events where you have to make small talk with people, consider hosting the event. By you being the host, you are the go-to person and it forces people to come to you. Another option is to seek out public speaking events. Public speaking allows you to speak to a broader audience instead of talking to people one on one.

An introvert may consider having an extroverted partner to help you navigate in business. A famous example of this type of partnership is Steve Wozniak who is an introvert and Steve Jobs who is an extrovert. The pair started Apple Computers. Jobs managed marketing, while Wozniak focused primarily on product development.

We live in a society where we value being busy. Introverts will reach a point where they simply must shun others in favor of alone time. Resist the temptation to see your urge for alone time as a weakness. The alone time you need is the air introverts breathe. This alone time will recharge you and restore your energy.

7 | ELIMINATE TIME-WASTERS

D istractions can get you off-focus from living out your dream. Before you know it, two hours have passed and you have been scrolling down the pages of a complete stranger's profile on social media. The time you spend being curious about the life of a so-called "influencer"or other stranger is valuable time you can spend being productive. You can use this time to pursue your dream. This is precious time you can never get back, so use it wisely.

With the rise of social media and people's desire to "follow" others, it is easy to become mesmerized watching other people become successful. I am fascinated when people tell me that they have been following a particular celebrity. There is a level of enjoyment in seeing someone grow their brand from a few followers to over 1 million followers. Why not use this same enjoyment by spending the time to fulfill your life's purpose?

Here are some common time-wasters to avoid:

Time-Waster #1. Looking for Money in all the Wrong Places
Decide if you need money or wisdom.

For months, I dreamed about someone bequeathing me lots of money to start my business. I thought that if

THE CLASSY HUSTLE

I received a lump sum of money all my problems would be solved. As I pondered this desire, an opportunity presented itself, and before long, my dreams almost became my reality. A colleague of mine was dating a guy who she introduced me to. He was "a fast-talker" and wanted to learn more about what I did. Our initial meeting resulted in a follow-up call from him. He told me about a group of venture capitalists he knew. He said that these people were incredibly wealthy and were looking to give away grants to minority business owners. He wanted to send them my business plan.

I thought that was going to be the answer to my financial struggles. I had to work fast to write up an astonishing business plan because he said that there needed to be a quick turnaround and the deadline was approaching. I wanted to secure this financing opportunity, so I emailed him the business plan and waited for a response. I followed up with an email to ensure that he received it. After a few days, he responded with confirmation that he received my correspondence and was awaiting a response from the investors. I waited for another reply. Crickets.... I never received a response from him again. I finally accepted the fact that I had been bamboozled.

Looking back at that experience, I now realize that my naivete got the best of me. If I received the lump sum of money I was anticipating, I would have missed valuable lessons. I was not ready to handle such a large sum of money in those early stages of owning my business. In hindsight, missing out on that "opportunity" allowed me to watch my business grow one dollar at a time. Until then, I did not understand the power of seeing one dollar grow at a time. This would eventually equate to my business growing to over $1 million dollars over a few years. I now understand the power of "eating slow and getting full". This expression was such a powerful lesson that my business-owner-friend shared with me.

Going after quick money is nothing more than a time-waster. If these "venture capitalist investors" invested in me, there's a good chance that I wouldn't be a business owner like I am now. The grant could have come with a contingency that they get to own a percentage of my business. It really could have been an offer that was too good to be true.

Time-Waster #2 Looking for Love in all the Wrong Places

Even after my hurtful and gruesome divorce, I knew that I wanted to find love again. I would say out loud that I am someone's wife and someone's mother. Reminding myself of my worth helped me to date with intention, specifically the intention to get married! I knew that because I was newly single and living in a new city, dating the wrong man could be a huge distraction in my endeavor to start a business. This knowledge was further confirmed after a conversation with an old acquaintance. As a recent graduate from esthetics school, she wanted to speak to me about her new career. While catching up, she explained that she had not reached the pinnacle of her singing career because she had spent several years chasing men while being otherwise unproductive. She was a talented musician, and I assumed that her move to Georgia would have catapulted her career. Instead, her insatiable desire to be in a relationship impeded her growth. She was now pursuing a new career as an esthetician. I felt that her story was a warning to me and showed me the importance of staying focused on going after my dream.

THE CLASSY HUSTLE

Her warning to me rang in the back of my head every time a suitor showed interest in me. I would think about her delay in pursuing her life's purpose. Along my path, I would meet interesting people who would share dating advice. I even had people question why I was so motivated to finance my business on my own. One person openly challenged my decision to operate independently. She wanted to show me how I could exchange sex for money. She said that because I was attractive I could date several men and get money from each of them to finance my business venture.

She spoke with conviction and from experience. She decided to demonstrate how she got money from the younger guys she dated. She wanted to prove the efficacy of her belief system. So, she started making phone calls to some of her suitors. When each one picked up, she demonstrated to me how to ask them for money.

I realized in that instant that I was operating my business on my own and in faith. It has been said that if you don't know where you're going, any road will take you there. If I started compromising my standards, the road she was recommending would have not led me to where I wanted to go. I had to remind myself of my belief, that I am someone's wife and someone's mother. I was born with a unique vision and for a specific purpose.

Six years later, the same advisor walked into my school to "surprise" me. This time, she brought her 26-year-old recently-divorced daughter with her. Her daughter was at a crossroads. She told her daughter about my entrepreneurial journey and my humble beginnings. She asked me what I would tell my 26-year-old self, So, I took a journey down memory lane. I gave her some nuggets of what I learned during that season of my life.

She was able to respect my journey as an entrepreneur. Choosing to do things the upright way doesn't always lead to accolades. But in this instance, I was able to see the fruits of my labor. She respected my classy hustle.

After two-and-a-half years of being in business, I was introduced to my husband. We met at a Thanksgiving dinner and were married one year later. He was not afraid to pursue my heart and endured my interrogations. He had then and still has a way of balancing me out. He showed me unconditional love and embraced my entrepreneurial spirit. Choosing to wait until my business was established and not getting sidetracked was the perfect move because it led me to him. It led us to each other.

Time-Waster #3 Spending Your Time in all the Wrong Places

Social media can be a huge distraction. If you find yourself with too little time on your hands, analyze how much time you are spending on social media. You can better use this time planning for your business. A lot of people complain about not having enough time in the day. Analyze where you spend your time and you will likely notice how much time you waste scrolling down other people's pages.

There are ways you can use your smartphone to track how much time you spend on social media. For example, I have a reminder set up in my phone to alert me when I have been on Instagram for 15 minutes. As soon as the reminder pops up, I immediately start limiting my time on this platform.

How much time I spend on social media is completely up to me. You can not get time back once it is gone, so spend it wisely. By eliminating time-wasters, you will gain the valuable time you need to pursue your dream.

8 | THE INVISIBLE LIFE

One of the hardest things about appreciating humble beginnings is that the grind to getting to your destination is not always glamorous. We live for instant gratification. We want it now and when now takes some time to get there, it is easy for frustration to set in. The journey to entrepreneurship can be lonely, time consuming, slow and humbling. Everyone's journey is different. While you are waiting, it is going to be important to build the right foundation.

DELAY DOES NOT MEAN DENIAL

The idea that delay does not mean denial has always resonated with me because I have always worked so hard to share my dreams with others. Although I was making moves, I was not seeing results as quickly as I wanted.

I call the process of working behind the scenes, training and preparing for life as an entrepreneur the "invisible life". This training and preparation is essential to the success of any entrepreneur. This training speaks of things not seen to the public eye and are not always spoken of. While you are in training, it is important to be selective with whom you share your dreams.

While I was waiting on approval for my school, I grew irritated. I figured if it was taking so long then I needed to consider doing something else. I shared my frustration with a skincare educator. Her words were fire. She told me that I need to be spending this time studying. She saw through my lack of participating in my skincare classes that I needed to know more. She told me that I needed to become an expert at my trade instead of a novice. I took her words to heart and started studying more about skincare.

Once the school received it's approval, I started teaching skincare classes. I became amazed at how much I knew when people asked me questions. The words spoken to me by my skincare educator prepared me for what was coming next. She had the insight to see what I was unable to see. I trusted that she knew best, and I made it a weekly habit to study. I needed to master my knowledge of esthetics to be able to teach to the magnitude I was expecting from my students.

Recently, I heard Duma Alphonse say on an Instagram post not to despise the 9-to-5 grind. What you do from 9-to-5 is your employer's time, but what you do from 5-to-9 is your time. Too many people complain about not having enough time, but really, they are often not using their time wisely. People are so relieved to get off of work that when they have their 5-to-9 time, they do not spend their time productively. For example, spending time on social media, lazing at happy hours or drinking to excess is unproductive. Many people are looking at the lives of people they admire instead of making moves to live the life they desire. When you start maximizing your 5-to-9 grind, your 9-to-5 job will serve its purpose of providing for you and your family. When you start maximizing your time from 5-to-9, you will see the manifestation of your dream.

WHAT ARE YOU READING?

There is an expression that "leaders are readers". I love reading, and from reading, I found out what makes people successful. During the beginning stages of entrepreneurship, reading saved me. There is so much valuable information in books. One of the things that I learned from all of my reading is that the secrets of the rich are found in books through reading. This information is passed on from generation to generation. Being illiterate impoverishes you.

While living the invisible life, the most helpful books were about my mindset, my thoughts. If I were to summarize what separates "the haves" from the "have-nots", it would be the mindset of the individual. Without the right mindset and the willingness to challenge your thoughts, you will falter at the first sign of an obstacle. Too many people quit too soon.

DON'T QUIT TOO SOON

Florence Mae Chadwick was a long distance swimmer. In 1957, she set out to swim 26 miles between Catalina Island and the California coastline. She prepared to swim this distance. She even had small boats nearby to watch out for sharks in the event she got hurt or grew tired. She swam for 15 hours and then a thick fog set in obscuring her view. She continued for one more hour and then decided to pull out of the race. After sitting in the boat, she found out that she had only been one mile away from finishing.

Two months later, Chadwick tried again. This time she was more prepared, as she spent time studying the course more closely. She kept a mental image of the shoreline as she swam, and despite the fog, succeeded in reaching Catalina. She prepared differently this time.

I love hearing about success stories. But, I love hearing about the ones who failed and got back up again even more. During her first attempt, Chadwick recognized that she quit right before the finish line. But, she did not allow that to be the end of her story, instead she used that race as a learning experience. Have you given up too soon? Are you about to quit right before the finish line? You are most likely only one mile away from the finish line.

HAVING THE RIGHT MINDSET

Some years back, I went to a three-day seminar about real estate investment. The first four hours of the workshop dealt with having the right mindset. Folks around me were so irritated about the seminar that they walked out. They walked out while the presenter was speaking about the thought process. Instead, they wanted him to get right into real estate investing. After the first half of the session, we left for lunch. When we came back to the seminar, the presenter explained that it was his strategy to be intentional about starting off speaking about having the right mindset to eliminate those with negative thinking. The presenter did a great job at this. So, if you only wanted the information on real estate investments, you had to wait. You could not get the information you came for without first addressing your mindset. I learned some valuable information from this seminar. I realized the importance of having the right mindset. Without it, you will not be able to sustain the uncertainties of real estate investing.

THE 5-YEAR ITCH

There is an expression that experience is the best teacher. But, that only applies when you have experience. What happens when you don't have experience? How does one go about getting it? When I first graduated from esthetics school, an opportunity presented itself to me. A friend of mine wanted me to buy her sister's salon and spa for a nominal cost of $100,000. I thought it was a great deal for a 4,000-square-foot salon and spa with hair stylists and a nail tech. I went to my school's owner to tell him about this exciting opportunity. I thought he would be ecstatic to hear the news. Instead, he looked at me and asked me what I knew about owning a business and if I had any experience doing it. My heart plummeted. I told him that I had a bachelor's degree in business, thinking that this would impress him. It didn't.

The school owner explained to me the importance of mastering my craft. In those seven minutes of speaking, he dropped nuggets of wisdom upon me. I savored his words because those words were life-changing. He explained that I needed to have a minimum of five years experience to own a salon and spa. He even encouraged me to go back to school to become a hair stylist if I wanted to own a salon. He asked what I thought I'd be left with if everyone walked out on me at once. It was his way of telling me that I don't own people. Whoa!!! These were points I didn't even consider. Everyone could walk out and I would be left with nothing but stuff! I felt defeated, and my spirit was deflated. But, I thanked him for his advice.

The five years he spoke of were essential to the success of my business. Five years goes by fast, and I learned that in five years you cannot master a craft.

You can become well-versed in it but not a master of it. Many experts say that it takes 10,000 hours of practice to master your craft.

I started my business six years from the conversation I had with my school owner. I am so glad that I waited and listened to him. After five years of being in business, I was able to show my gratitude to him and his wife in person. I let him know that I listened to his advice. He was curious to know what advice I was speaking of, so I told him that I was referring to him telling me to wait five years to start my business so I could learn more about my craft. He looked at me in amazement as he asked if I knew how many other people he had given that advice to. I can imagine that there were countless people and most of them did not listen. I'm sure that there were countless people who wished that they would have. I am so glad that I was one of the few who heeded his advice.

TRAINING DAYS

To get more experience in your industry while you are waiting to open your own business, you can get a part-time job working for a company in that same industry. For example, if you want to start a coffee shop, consider working for Starbucks for a few years. Learn every facet of their business model. Take note of how they personalize their service and what it is about the experience they provide that makes them stand out from their competitors. Learn every detail you can from how they change their trash cans to the efficiency of their drive-through line. If you frowned at the thought of studying how they change the trash cans, you may want to re-evaluate your mindset. In the beginning stages of your business, you will do every job for it, including changing trash cans. I still do it to this day!

When I worked as the director of education, I wore dress suits and heels to work daily. If the spa equipment would break, I would put in the request to order more. My corporate education manager did not like this process. He decided to change the ordering process to make it more rigorous. To get approval for new equipment, I would have to take pictures of the broken equipment, and if I did not know what was wrong with the broken equipment, I had to troubleshoot it. This process landed me on the cold, concrete floor. It required me taking off my heels, sitting on the floor (with my suit on) and turning over the machines. I resented doing it, as I felt that this job was beneath me. But it was not, this process was preparing me. Now that I have my own school with lots of spa equipment, I am able to troubleshoot and repair any equipment that stops working. I laugh every time I fix a piece of equipment, as I am reminded of my training days and my humble beginnings.

WHAT'S IN YOUR HAND?

While working behind the scenes, you will see results over time. Some of the results were seriously unimaginable. You may grow up doing something you think is trivial like gardening. After several years of gardening, you may realize that you have a green thumb. Because of this knack, you may want to start your own business. In turn, you take care of large corporations' plants. Gardening actually served a greater purpose. It prepared you for your business venture.

Do not despise small things. In the world of InstaPot, InstaGram, InstaSuccess, we get used to processes happening fast. It's easy to wonder why things take so long to manifest. People have no idea how many years "Instagram-famous" models have been practicing their craft. While something may appear to be an overnight success, I can assure you, it was not. Very few people will tell you about their grind and what they had to go through to get to where they are.

Here is a secret, the less you know, the less you do. We live in a time when information is fast and easy to come by. You can pretty much Google anything you want to know whenever you want it. This information is available to you within a split second. Having information alone serves no purpose, you need to apply it to make it useful.

LIVING A PRINCIPLED LIFE

The invisible life is for those who want to start a self-sustaining business. You want your business to last so that you can either grow it to sell it or keep it for generations to come. The invisible life puts into practice selfless principles that are motivated with the intention of helping others. Thus, you put in the work to ensure that your business thrives and survives. You implement principles, such as, "eat slow and you'll get full". "Master your craft by working in your field for a minimum of five years before you start your own business". "The dream is not just for me".

Once you start challenging your thinking, you will recognize some things. You will recognize how many of your thoughts are not truly serving you. Once you change the way you think, you will view success differently. You will become appreciative of changing the trash cans at Starbucks. Because you know that one day you will own your own business. You will bring a change of clothes to work knowing that the equipment needs to be fixed. You will fix the machines with excitement knowing that one day you will have your own school.

Start looking at events in your life as training instead of difficulties. Do everything with excellence from 9-to-5 knowing that your 5-to-9 hours are yours to prepare for your next move. Stop feeling resentment about working for someone else. Use your time wisely, and work the same way you want someone to work for you.

Recently, someone asked me if I could ever work for someone else if anything ever happened to my business. While I would not want to, I would. I would work for someone else with the same spirit of excellence I have working for myself. Don't get it twisted, if you are half-stepping working for "the man", you will half-step working for yourself.

Entrepreneurship is a daily grind. Even when people are working for you, you are still working behind the scenes. You work to ensure your business is running smoothly and is self-sustaining. Your goal will be to have the people who work for you helping to propel your business. Until this day happens, your business success is predicated on what you have put in place — even if it means changing the trash can every now and then.

ARE YOU WHAT YOU'RE LOOKING FOR?

Our pastors, Tim and LeChelle Johnson preached a series about relationships. They posed the question that I am going to pose to you, "Are YOU what You're Looking for?" Are you what you are expecting from other peo-

THE CLASSY HUSTLE

ple? I have always worked hard and have been working since I was 14. When I was young, I enjoyed working to make money. As I became an adult, I considered myself a hard worker. I learned that I am a multitasker, and I liked making money for my work. So, when I started my own business, I worked even harder for myself. Since I have always been a hard worker, it was easy for me to ask that from others as I grew my team. At times, I even did my employees' jobs.

I can answer YES, that I am what I am looking for when I make hiring decisions. Because I am a hard worker, I expect others to work hard. Because I walk in integrity and truth, I expected others to walk in integrity and truth. I am what I am looking for. If you are lazy, dishonest and shady, do not expect your employees to work for you while you do nothing. It will not work.

One time when I was at a restaurant, an employee of the establishment talked to me about pursuing his own business even though he was on the job and being paid by the employer. He was supposed to be working but instead was talking to me and my husband about his dream. He had no respect for the employer's time. I watched as this person talked, and I questioned his work ethic. I wondered what he was doing from 5-to-9. If I were a betting person, I would say that he was resentful about working a 9-to-5 job, and during his 5-to-9 time, was doing nothing to prepare for his own business. Upon a return to the restaurant, I learned that he was terminated. Our waitress told us that the owner noticed that he spent his time talking to customers instead of working and fired him.

WHO ARE YOU AROUND?

The invisible life is surrounded by like-minded people. At first, you may not have many people with the same mindset to associate with. As you continue to grow, you will begin to attract like-minded individuals who will be drawn to you. To test if these people are real or fake, ask questions like, what books they read and what they do in their spare time. Make sure that the words they speak match their actions before sharing your dream.

Successful people associate with other successful people. You cannot make a seven-figure salary by associating with people who make five figures. As you grow, your associations will shift. I am not saying to stop talking to all your friends and acquaintances who are making less than what you make. But, I am saying that those in your closest circle must have the same mindset as you. The mindset must be similar in understanding what success looks like. You will start to have the same views on money, relationships and goals.

One day, I was feeling overwhelmed with my business. During our breakfast, I had an emotional breakdown around those in my inner-circle. They gave me a few minutes to cry, comforted me and then began to speak into my life. Within minutes, they came up with a plan to help ease my responsibilities. I wiped my tears, got in my car to go to work and developed a mental action plan. Within five hours, I called our HR team, they created a position and had the job posted online within two days. We hired someone within the month for this valuable role. What if my inner-circle had encouraged me to shut down my business because I was having a bad day?

It is important to surround yourself with people who can

speak life into your future. They will be able to see that what you are going through is temporary. Never make a permanent decision based on temporary factors. Too many times permanent decisions are made because we are having a bad day. Wise council can help you see through the fog. I was in no position to make a permanent decision. My friends were able to see that I needed a full-time office manager. That was all. There was no need to shut down the business when all I needed was to hire help. I was only one mile away from the finish line. My friends were able to help me navigate through the fog to completion. Carefully select your inner-circle. These people can be some of your greatest assets or your worst nightmares. Choose wisely.

ONE DAY THEY ARE GOING TO SAY THEY KNEW YOU!

When I worked in corporate America, I used to survive on the thought that one day "they" were going to say that they knew me. I was in a dark place.The criticism I received for being an effective leader caused others to isolate me. Professional colleagues are just as vulnerable to peer pressure as teenagers are, and this was the position I was in. I saw that it was easier for people to believe the lies spoken about me than to seek out truth about my true character.

While being isolated and feeling alone, I thought to myself that one day those people are going to say that they knew me. That thought actually brought me comfort. I knew that I was designed for greatness! Because of the greatness in my life, these people were nothing more than stepping stones for getting me where I needed to go. I knew I would move on with my life with very few memories about these people. They served their purpose. I knew where I was going, they would eventually say, I knew Tessa!

Don't be afraid to walk in such integrity that others around you grow uncomfortable. Don't be afraid to raise the standard so that those around you will have to work harder. Set the tone but never conform to complacency. Complacent people do not set records and do not stand out from the rest. Be the one who leaves the company so that your colleagues will say they knew you!

9 | THE IMPORTANCE OF MENTORSHIP

Lately, we have seen an increase in vision board parties at the beginning of the year. On the first of the year, I attended one of these parties. It's a great way to start the new year. Before working on the vision boards, the host had several keynote speakers come to speak on various topics, including time management skills, healthy lifestyles and the importance of mentorship. All of the attendees were asked to write down the names of three people who could help them reach their goals.

A few days after the event, I had breakfast with my inner-circle friends. One of them mentioned receiving an influx of calls from people wanting to have lunch with her to pick her brain. She questioned why so many people were reaching out to her at once. I told her about the vision board party I attended and the practice they encouraged. The light bulb went off for her, they wanted her to help them reach their goals. She scheduled times with each person. One person scheduled a call, throughout which she chattered about four different topics. When my friend, with whom she requested the meeting, tried to interject, the lady kept talking rather than stopping to listen to my friend give her expert advice.

I am baffled by the fact that people who want to associate with successful people want to spend that time talking instead of listening. Most people want to be heard but do not want to listen to sound advice from trusted people. So, before moving forward with soliciting the help of a mentor, you must be receptive to and willing to heed their advice. Highly successful people do not have the time or energy to waste on people who are not teachable. There are reasons why they are successful. Here's a word of advice: Learn how to be quiet in the presence of people who know more than you. You will be amazed at what nuggets of wisdom you can take away from their experience. You may even find the answers you have been seeking.

THE DIFFERENCE BETWEEN PROFESSIONALS AND ENTREPRENEURS

There is a difference between an entrepreneur and a professional. As an entrepreneur, I get excited about taking risks. A friend of mine who's an accountant, told me that she has to be careful when giving entrepreneurs advice. She recognizes that she is pessimistic at times and does not like taking risks. Risk is the very thing that drives entrepreneurs to become successful, and it is exactly what she cautions against. She is a professional accountant (CPA) meanwhile I am a serial entrepreneur. Know the difference.

MENTORS

The history of mentorship dates back to 3,000 years ago. The history and concept of mentorship involves the professional training of a pupil by a more experienced peer. When referring to a "mentor" it was the name of the person who acted as guardian, advisor, teacher and friend.

THE CLASSY HUSTLE

My first mentor was my father. My father quit his blue-collar job to pursue a career as an entrepreneur. During his hayday, he achieved great success owning his own insurance business. I grew up watching him work hard and build a team. I always knew that I wanted to follow in his footsteps of entrepreneurship.

I knew when I advanced to becoming a manager of more than 25 employees that I needed help. There was no way I was going to become successful in that role without the help of a mentor. For me to be successful, I needed to be groomed. I thought about who I could trust to mentor me. At the time, I preferred having a successful female of the same ethnicity. It was important that we shared some of the same spiritual beliefs. The mentor's name came to me while I was thinking and meditating. I sent her a request to schedule a time with her, and she agreed. I made sure to be properly dressed and to arrive on time. I did not want to miss this opportunity, as I knew that her time, wisdom and expertise was invaluable.

Our first meeting was a bit intimidating. She invited me to her home. It was a beautiful, regal-looking four-level condominium. We went to the third floor where her office was located. I sat across from her bookshelf where she displayed the accolades and awards she received over her 30-year career. I was mesmerized. She was famous in her world, and I was honored to be in her presence. She took my request of mentorship seriously. We discussed the details of her prolific career and then she transitioned our focus to my needs. She put her reader glasses on the tip of her nose indicating she was ready to begin questioning me. She asked very poignant and direct questions about the three areas I most wanted to expand my business and what my business model was.

I am so glad I prepared for this meeting because her questions were pensive. I answered her questions effortlessly because I prepared. I had written out where I wanted to go and I did not want to waste her time. After passing her series of questions, she agreed to mentor me. While she did not come out and say that, her next steps indicated her intent.

We met at least twice a month. With each session, she helped me stay focused and gave me direction. When my mentor first started working with me, I was an employee and needed help with managing my faculty and staff. As time passed, I left my 9-to-5 to pursue my 5-to-9 entrepreneurial endeavors.

A mentor is a resource and can show you what to do. Most mentors are extremely selective in who they chose to mentor, which makes sense because mentors have mastered their craft and know what it takes to be successful. They are valuable in helping you reach your goals and holding you accountable.

Throughout my life, I received many words about me becoming a multimillionaire. I did not know what people saw in me that gave them that notion, but it was being spoken a lot. I was not impressed or excited. I actually was afraid of it happening before I was ready to receive it. So I prayed and asked God not to allow me to become a millionaire until I knew what the money was for.

I always heard that money magnifies who you are, and I was still trying to figure out who I was. I did not know what I would do with a million dollars. I believe that God honored my request. He allowed me to meet several multimillionaires whom I could interview. I was able to have conversations with them and ask questions.

One of the questions I always posed was, "what is money for?" I knew the obvious reason was to pay bills and keep a roof over my head. But, what was I to do with millions of dollars? I grew up very materialistic and saw money as a tool to gain more possessions. I was becoming content with what I had and was becoming more concerned about my character. After some years of asking, I finally got my answer, which helped me to accept my financial increase. Money is for helping others and helps to open doors of opportunity. Of course, I received other answers, but this answer resonated with me. I saw purpose in the increase of my finances, causing me to plan with a purpose.

I have had many mentors along my journey. Some served one purpose and others served several purposes. Throughout this book, you have heard me speak about the mentors who have spoken into my life.

During my pursuit of entrepreneurship, there was one mentor who helped to develop me. I refer to her often, as she is one of the people I am accountable to. Her accolades precede her, her character follows her and she walks in truth and integrity. She believes in giving back. I was honored that she selected me as her protege. She made it very clear that several people asked her to mentor them who she did not choose to work with. I was glad to be among the chosen. Her mentorship helped me to develop my character. You become who you associate with.

The one thing I realized as I grew older was that people have the ability to see past what someone else is portraying. The fact that my mentor chose me as her protege was a testament to her confidence in me. Most trusted advisors, including coaches and mentors, will not do the work for you. That is not their job. Their job is to provide you with useful information. They provide resources and material that will help you help yourself. This information should catapult you to the next level. If your advisor is not challenging you and making you uncomfortable, he or she is not doing the job.

COACHES

Coaches are different from mentors. While they have similarities, they have different responsibilities. A mentor provides support for career growth and interpersonal skill development and provides guidance along the way. The relationship is respectful but can be more informal than a relationship with a business coach.

Business coaches focus on specific skills and development goals in a particular industry. They break elements of the industry into concrete tasks that need to be completed over a set period of time. Hire a coach if you want help reaching a specific goal in the industry in which the coach is an expert.

For many business owners, identifying and prioritizing goals is a big challenge. Business coaches address this challenge by helping businesses identify what the goal is. Once this goal is identified, the business coach can help you focus on your goals in the order of their importance.

Business coaches follow a more formal, structured approach to resolving issues. They manage specific aspects of the job. A great business coach challenges the status quo. One of my business coach's challenges the status quo in everything he does. Because of his approach, he is an extremely successful real estate coach investor.

Because he challenges the status quo, he causes me to challenge the beliefs that limit me. There is nothing wrong with someone challenging your beliefs. Keep in mind they are just that, beliefs. If you are "stuck" and haven't been able to get past a particular sales goal or a specific point in your career, consider why. Hire a business coach.

To help me in writing this book, I hired a coach who has written several books. He took me to places through the writing process that I could not have taken myself. He was able to help me in this way because he has experience in writing and publishing books. He knew something I did not know. His knowledge was invaluable to me. The valuable resources he provided helped me finish this book on time. I have been writing the words for this book for over seven years, but I wrote the complete book in four months. He taught me how to properly structure the book and gave me the focus and intentionality I needed to write it.

You need to have trusted advisors to help get you through your new experiences. These advisors will help you navigate the challenges of life. It is incredibly important to not despise the difficult obstacles you encounter. These challenges can teach you valuable lessons. Quiet yourself long enough to listen.

10 | YOU ARE YOUR GREATEST INVESTMENT

I choose ME. If I were to summarize what happened to allow me to finish writing this book, it would say, I chose ME. Choosing you can be difficult, especially when you are a giving and thoughtful person. But, by not choosing yourself, it will lead to burnout and having unfulfilled dreams. I realized that my management style was becoming too nurturing. I wanted to fix everyone's problems. So, instead of my employees working while on the clock, I was counseling them. I was not seeing the fruit from their paycheck, instead I was experiencing burnout. I was drained from advising and coaching people for free. Meanwhile, those around me were benefiting from me. I was getting too emotionally involved in the lives of others.

I have spent several years in therapy. Therapy is one of the greatest tools ever and one of the greatest gifts you can give yourself. Since we are made of mind, body and spirit, it is crucial to make sure our minds are right. I tell my husband all the time that I'm not crazy because my therapist told me so. While I am being a bit facetious, healing from your trauma leads to emotional increase and wholeness.

BECOMING WHOLE

When you become whole, you want others to become whole. The problem is that it takes work to become whole. I was willing to put in the work for myself, whereas others wanted to reap from my wholeness. So, I was always being drained by trying to help. This had to change. I had to have a paradigm shift in how I viewed others. Instead of seeing them as powerless and needing to be fixed, I saw them as being powerful. They had the power to change if they wanted to.

I do not think you can invest in yourself until you know that you are worth investing in. How do you value yourself?

FIND YOUR VALUE AND WORTH
I struggled for years in knowing my value and worth. I wanted acceptance from others and I wanted to fit in. Because I was a "little different" I defined my worth as others saw me. I had limited beliefs in what I was capable of achieving. By putting in the work, I started to peel off layers of the onion. The outer layer represented how I wanted others to see me. I peeled that layer off. The next layer represented how I really saw myself, that part was a little painful. I realized that I received negative words spoken by other people. This wasn't really who I was, it was what I accepted as truth, so it was a lie. I denounced those lies. I was left with the core of the onion, which represented who I really was.

I asked myself questions about who I really am, what I like and what makes me tick. Once I was able to answer these questions with certainty, I was able to see who Tessa really is. Now, I work hard to show up being who I am and not who others want to see. Because I know who I am, I do not need others to define or validate me.

INVEST IN YOUR FUTURE

One of the challenges I have with enrolling students at my school is the tuition cost. People who do not value their worth struggle with spending money on themselves. We are a cash-pay school and do not offer financial aid from the government. We do have extended payment plan options that are affordable for many.

Students have up to one year from their start date to pay their tuition, yet still the cost seems too great for some prospective students. I have observed that they struggle to spend money investing in their future, but they have no problems investing in material things. They say they can not afford the tuition, but I notice them carrying the latest luxury bags or wearing expensive hair extensions.

After my observations, I complete my tour and recognize that they are not ready. They are not ready to invest in themselves and are not ready to be students in my program. They would rather indulge in temporary pleasures instead of investing in lifelong goals.

When I first started the school, I had a prospective student interview me. She had researched the industry and wanted to ensure she got her money's worth. She had saved up enough money from working at Disney Japan to pay her tuition in full. Her questions let me know that she was serious about her enrollment and her success in our program. She enrolled and finished our program in five months.

While in school, she got a job as a receptionist for a waxing studio. Once she received her license, she transitioned from receptionist to doing waxing services. She came back to the school after five months of working there and told me that she had truly received a return on her investment within four months of graduating. I was amazed at her level of maturity at just 21 years of age. She understood that the tuition she paid in full was an investment in her future. She paid the cost upfront knowing that she was going to reap a reward.

Truth be told, I learned from her what "investing in yourself" looks like. When I was 18 years old, I went to a four-year university because I was told to go, not because I was investing in myself. I looked at college as what you do after high school to land a job. I never had discussions with my parents about working while I was in school to pay for my tuition. Instead, I was told to go to a school in Ohio, where I am from, so that I could receive grants and loans. I knew that I could not go out of state because the tuition would be too expensive. I was ignorant about money so I took out loans so that I could live. I took out the greatest amount so that I could receive a reimbursement check and then I spent the money on frivolous things. I knew that one day I would have to pay it back but chose to live for the moment. Had I received more advice on money, I would not have made such bad choices.

I realized that financial illiteracy got me into a situation that took decades for me to get out of. I saw student loans as a bill that would eventually get paid, but there was no urgency attached to them. I took out the longest time to repay my loans, as they were a non-factor. I did not consider the interest and how much I would actually be paying back. Financial illiteracy had me making unwise decisions. Any time I felt like I needed more money, I would defer my loans or put them in financial forbearance. I was simply delaying having to pay them back.

INVEST IN YOU

It takes courage to invest in yourself. The hungrier you are, the more you will learn from your training. There are many ways that you can invest in yourself, including:

- Reading books
- Listening to audio readings
- Attending live seminars
- Listening to podcasts
- Attending webinar trainings
- Investing in a business coach

Start with what you can afford, for example, buying a book. Set a goal to read one book a month, and do not buy another book until you have finished reading the previous one. As you progress in your thinking, sign up for a LIVE event. There is nothing more magnetic than a LIVE event. The energy you get from the speaker and being around other like-minded people is resounding. Start off by scheduling one live event per quarter and gradually increase to one event every month.

As you begin putting these practices in place, you will notice a difference in your thinking. You will start to figure out ways to invest in yourself even more. You will start to eliminate expenses that are not serving you. You will stop spending so much time on mindless activities like heavy consumption of television watching. Use your time more wisely. As a word of caution, pace yourself. I have been guilty of being an extremist and trying to do everything at once. There is no way you can master everything overnight. I like to say that I was a bunny at a fast pace whereas my husband was a turtle. My overzealous nature was starting to wear him out. Over time, we managed to balance each other out.

THE CLASSY HUSTLE

Some of the live events I attended had nothing to do with my trade of esthetics. I have participated in several classes on topics like real estate, stock trading and book writing. I wanted to learn everything I could about different industries and topics. I did not want to limit my options. Years later, I started making more money and needed a financial manager. By attending the stock classes, I understood the basics of investing. When I met with my financial wealth manager, I was able to converse with him about investments. I understood stock options, mutual funds and government bonds.

I knew that one day we would outgrow the space in my school. The real estate course taught me about different ways to buy commercial property. Now that we are about to buy a building, I am able to discuss options and terms with my commercial realtor.

I always desired to write a book and have been an avid journaler for years. Writing helped me express my excitement, anger and confusion at times. When I go back and read my old journals, I am reminded of my journey. I am reminded of the experiences that hurt me, shaped me and define who I am now. I had no idea that when I started journaling as a child I was preparing to be a writer. I was finding my voice through journaling.

After attending the book-writing class, I understood that writing a book helps in many ways. Writing a book sets you apart as an authority figure, even if your topic is about collecting trash.

You investing in yourself will give you experiences you dreamed about. You will start to meet people who matter and will make a difference in your journey. When I started taking LIVE classes, I met all kinds of people.

After my book-writing class, many of the participants formed a think tank. This core group of people were diverse. We had a former New York police officer, a naturopath, realtor and office manager. While we all had diverse backgrounds, we had one thing in common, we all wanted to write a book. We all had different motivations for writing a book and each one of us was willing to help each other in whatever way possible.

As my business began to grow, I needed a coach to help balance my various roles. I did not have a lot of money to invest, but wanted to start somewhere. I reached out to someone I knew and admired about having a lunch date. During our lunch date, she mentioned starting her coaching business. She expressed an interest in coaching me. I agreed to her coaching and we agreed on a set price. Looking back, I realize it was a pretty nominal price but a good start for the both of us. We focused our attention on me being too busy working inside the business. She gave me some strategies to ease my workload, as I was a newly-wedded bride. I incorporated these strategies and freed up some time within four months. During our final meeting, she told me that she was firing me as a client because I attained the goals we set. As specific needs came up, I continued hiring different coaches. I am a firm believer that you need people to hold you accountable. You need to have people push you further than where you can take yourself.

Even as parents, it is important that your children see you investing in yourself. When they see you happy and content as you are walking out your purpose, it encourages them to follow suit. I am amazed by how many children speak at our graduation ceremony about being proud of their parent. I have had children from ages six on up share their excitement on seeing their moms make the honor roll.

Children love coming to the school to be a model for their moms. They love doing their homework while their Mommies are doing their homework. It becomes a participatory activity where they get to spend valuable time with you. While in school, many of our graduates with children saw an increase in their children's grades. Your children watch what you do, more than listen to what you say. When they see you studying, practicing and improving yourself, it makes them want to do better. So don't think that you have to wait until your child graduates high school or leave your house to pursue your goal. What you do affects your child and family more than you will ever realize.

There is no one who can invest in you more than you. There is no one with your blueprint, your DNA and your fingerprints. When you start making the necessary steps to invest in you, you are going to meet someone special. If you are struggling in this area, you may need to spend some time seeking out additional help. This help can come from a certified, licensed therapist.

I must pause here. Be aware of who you seek counsel from. Your pastor, church member, family, girlfriends, male friends are not therapists. They are advisors or confidants. leave them there. To deal with lifelong trauma, hangups and repetitive habits, we must get to the root cause. Peel back that onion in a safe and healing environment. Get to the core of what's going on with you. Find out what is blocking you from experiencing increase. The money that you spend on getting the help you need will be one of the greatest investments you make for you.

While I recognize that mental illness is real, it does not define you. It simply means that you are unbalanced in certain areas. I am not an expert in mental illness nor am I a certified, licensed therapist. I am an avid believer in the power of therapy from a trusted, certified, licensed therapist. Too many people are seeking help from the wrong people and getting messed up in the process. Get the help you need to walk in freedom. When you know your worth, you will recognize that you are worth investing in.

No matter your circumstance, it is important to know that the dream is not just for you. As a matter of fact, the dream is bigger than you. In choosing you, you are choosing a life worth living, a life of freedom.

Be tenacious and never give up. You are the original manuscript! Have you considered how many people would be affected by you not pursuing your dream? Surround yourself with like minded people, people who will hold you accountable. People who will motivate you to pursue your dreams. Dare to choose you and dare to live your fondest dreams!

AFTERWORD

I truly hope you enjoyed reading my first book, "The Classy Hustle™". This book has been in the making since 2006, the year I moved from Cincinnati, Ohio to Orlando, Florida. I knew I wanted to write a book but did not know how to formalize my words into a book format. I believe in the dream of entrepreneurship, and I believe in accountability. Although I am a self-driven person, it is always good having a coach to motivate me. My goal is to have people around me who will help me go further than where I can on my own. So, I live my life by being accountable to others. If you are interested in being coached by me, I would encourage you to visit my page at www.TessaEBoyd.com. If the words written in this book resonated with you, I invite you to follow me.

Twitter: @TessaEBoyd
Instagram: @TessaEBoyd
Facebook: @TessaEBoyd

To schedule a speaking engagement with me, please visit our website at www.TessaEBoyd.com, click on the link, speaking engagements.

21115509R00064

MW00604124

from copy of Stood

Bellows!

success in going

there at 6'9th?

James?

Cups to Gallons

How to Profit More by Launching a Very Lucrative Catering Business

By Stacey and Dave Riska,
Your Cups to Gallons Champions

Cups to Gallons
How to Profit More by Launching a Very Lucrative Catering Business

Published by Small Business Expertise Publishing
10319 Westlake Drive
#105
Bethesda, MD 20817

ISBN: 978-1-7322459-2-1

Cover design by Jim Saurbaugh

business in the United States or any other jurisdiction, is the sole responsibility of the purchaser or reader.

To our sons, Brandon and Stephen, who overflow with Aloha Spirit and gave us the inspiration to go from cups to gallons

Table of Contents

Foreword

I find it so interesting when a small business owner "discovers" a new way to take an ordinary business and, with a simple idea or seemingly simple twist, transform their business into a money machine! And yet, it is often the "head-slapping" simple ideas the rest of us marvel at. That is exactly how I came to meet and grow to admire and respect Stacey and Dave Riska.

This book will no doubt inspire and encourage you, but more importantly, it will also serve as a roadmap or blueprint on how to take an ordinary coffee or smoothie business and turn it into a business that you can fairly describe as a cash machine!

Stacey and Dave are the true definition of what it means to be inspiring entrepreneurs. They have started and grown many businesses. They've experienced the joy of success and also the gut-wrenching agony of crushing debt and loss. One evening, while pondering their bleak future based on the huge amount of debt they generated from their current businesses, they came to a realization: Simply selling more *cups* of coffee or smoothies – even with an increase of 50 percent – it would take an eternity to turn things around, if it could even be done at all.

The simple twist that solved their problem and eventually helped them become debt free – and highly profitable – was shifting from selling more "cups" to selling gallons! I know what you're likely thinking, "Yes, that sounds good, but I'm not a caterer!"

To that I say, "Well, neither were Dave and Stacey... and look at them now!"

The book you're holding tells the story of a simple twist in thinking and a willingness to try something new, and it might be the turning point you've been looking for. Hosting a few corporate events or private parties just might be the ticket to seeing a substantial increase not just in your gross revenue but also in your profits.

Stacey and Dave Riska took a struggling business, applied some simple yet effective strategies (that they share and describe in this book), and started earning more in three hours than they were making in a week. I encourage you to set aside your preconceived notions about "catering" and read this book with an open mind.

As Stacey and Dave share their proven strategies, ask yourself, "What if I did this in my business?"

Jim Palmer
The Dream Business Coach
www.getjimpalmer.com

Why Listen to Us?

First of all, we've been exactly where you are now... perhaps even worse. Our story started with a mid-life crisis. After owning an outsourcing business for 10 years in which we handled the back-office work for associations and nonprofits, Stacey woke up one day, had her mid-life crisis, and realized that, although she had a successful and profitable business, she needed something fun to do.

So what else would you do? Start a tropical-themed coffee and smoothie business. That's what we did.

We both had great ambitions – to take over the Washington D.C. metro area. And grow we did. In our first two years of business, we had two stores in Dulles Airport, a store in a mall, ten mobile tiki bars, and two food trucks. The growth was great. But then...

... it was crash and burn!

When the economy ground to a halt in 2008, so did we, painfully so.

No one was traveling, despite us paying the most expensive rents in the country. No one was going to the mall just to get a coffee or a smoothie. The concourses at Dulles seemed empty, and the travelers that passed by our stores weren't splurging for a smoothie.

We were – and we are not exaggerating this – $500,000 in debt! Yes, the number of zeroes there is not a typo. We were so broke, we didn't have enough money to buy the next week's inventory. How can you run a business like that? Those were very dark days, indeed.

> $500,000 in debt to a seven-figure profitable business. We did that and want to help you do the same!

Perhaps you can relate, and whether or not you may currently be in a similar situation, we were able to pull the business back up and out of the threatening flames of bankruptcy. In fact, **we went from $500,000 in debt to a seven-figure profitable business**. That's why you should listen to us... and keep reading!

How?

One five-letter word: *cater.*

We began to cater – serving multiple customers at one time and location – and it completely transformed our business. Instead of selling coffees and smoothies one cup at a time, we sold them by the gallon. What a game changer!

Now when we say, "sold by the gallon," we don't mean that literally. Throughout this book, we'll more clearly define what we mean by "selling by the gallon." In essence, it's the difference between making pennies and making dollars. Which would you rather do?

Unfortunately, way too many independent coffee, smoothie, juice bar, ice cream and/or dessert shop owners are selling by the cup, chained to a business they work "in" rather than working "on." That's why we're so passionate about helping them – and you – learn how to start catering, so you can go from pennies to dollars... aka cups to gallons.

This book provides the blueprint that will guide you through everything you need to know. You'll understand the exact steps to take to go from selling by the cup and instead sell by the gallon. Working less for a lot more money and having a business you love again will be a reality by following the steps we outline here. Grab a cup of coffee. You won't want to put this down until you finish it!

To your success,
Stacey and Dave

Chapter One:

Take Price Out of the Equation

You have the best products in town. You have the coolest store, too. People love to stop in, enjoy what you offer, and support their local business.

They're paying you $3.00, $4.00, maybe even $5.00 or $6.00 a cup... but you're still selling one... cup... at ... a... time!

How many cups do you have to sell to make $800.00? We'll save you the time to do the math. *It's: a lot!*

We're also willing to bet that you're not even making that much in your store, consistently and day after day. Why $800.00? Because that's our *average* catering job, and we do it in four hours with an average *net* profit margin at 75 percent!

Are you working four hours and putting $600.00 in your pocket? Most coffee, smoothie, juice bar, ice cream or dessert shop owners answer, "No!" We're guessing that if you're still reading, you have the same answer.

You may be thinking, "Well, I do catering. I sell 'to-go' boxes that can be picked up... or we'll even deliver." From our perspective, that's not the type of catering that will take you from cups to gallons – pennies to dollars. That's still selling by the cup.

Someone ordering that box of coffee has a value in their head about what it's worth and what they're willing to pay for it. If you tried selling that box of coffee for $800.00, you'd no doubt be laughed at, hung up on, and probably have pages and pages of negative reviews.

So, how then do you sell $800.00 worth of catering that people will happily pay without ever questioning your price?

You sell an experience, not a commodity.

Understand this concept, and it will completely transform your business.

A cup of coffee is a cup of coffee. A smoothie is a smoothie. Both are commodities and have an inherent value in someone's head of what they're worth and what they're willing to pay for it.

But what if instead of selling a cup of coffee or a smoothie, you sold an experience? Which would you prefer:

Staff person says, "Hey, What's up?"	Staff person greets you with a warm, "Aloha!"
Staff person wearing a standard collared shirt	"Tikitenders" wearing bright, floral Hawaiian shirts
Cup of coffee	"Taste of island perfection"
Smoothie	"Vacation in a cup!"
Hot chocolate	"Warmth of Aloha!"
Catering	"Ultimate Hawaiian Getaway without a 12-hour flight!"

The entries on the left are all commodities. Anyone can get that anywhere, and there's an inherent value in what they're willing to pay for a commodity.

The entries on the right create an experience. If you were interested in our smoothie catering services, this is what we'd say:

"We'll come out and set up a tiki bar where our professional 'tikitenders' blend gourmet, all-natural fresh fruit smoothies topped off with a Hawaiian parasol. No wonder people call us a 'vacation in a cup'!"

Now which would you rather have? A smoothie or a "vacation in a cup"?

In two simple sentences, we've painted a picture of what the *experience* is, and by doing so, it completely takes price out of the equation. At this point, people want it. Price is not the deciding factor.

> Create an experience rather than simply delivering a product!

They want something fun, something different, and because we're bringing it all to them, making it easy for them while also making them look great to their guests, they say "YES" to that $800 catering job without even thinking about it.

In your store, if you were to charge $20 or even $30 for a coffee or smoothie (or whatever you sell), you'd be laughed at and find your register empty. In a store setting, a cup of coffee is a cup of coffee, a smoothie is a smoothie, and people are only willing to spend so much for it. But when you follow the Cups to Gallons system as outlined in this book, you'll get that – and more – without the customer even realizing that's how much they're ultimately paying.

When catering is done correctly, price is never the determining factor.

Cups to Gallons, Pennies to Dollars:

- A cup of coffee or smoothie is just that, and you'll generate dollars rather than pennies by turning it into an experience instead.
- Imagine making $800.00 for four hours of work and putting $600.00 of that right in your pocket!
- When you sell a commodity, you will always be competing on price. When you create an experience, you take price right out of the equation.

Want to learn more about how to go from Cups to Gallons? Visit CupsToGallons.com.

Chapter Two:

"I'm Not a Caterer!"

"I'm not a caterer." Maybe that's what you're telling yourself right now. That was the misguided mindset we had as well, convinced we weren't caterers. We were at an event selling our coffees and smoothies, next to a Ben & Jerry's stand. We started talking with the owner, asking how business was. He said, "The store is barely covering costs, but I made mid-six figures last year with catering, working just a few hours a week." WOW! Light bulb moment. We were busting our humps doing whatever we could to sell "one more cup at a time."

We had never thought of ourselves as caterers. Maybe you're thinking the same thing. However, after that event, our lives completely changed. Since we were already going out and setting up at events, we had everything we needed to start catering. It just so happened that a few days after that light bulb moment, someone in the store asked us if we could provide smoothies for a birthday party she was having at her home. "Yes we can!"

Honestly, we had no idea what we were doing. We doubted ourselves. "We're not a caterer; should we really do this?" We had no idea how to price it. We didn't have any systems in place – what to offer, how to structure a menu, how to create a contract, etc. While we had done events like fairs, festivals, and community events, those were "selling" events, very different from catering. But we had said "yes," so we were now committed to figuring it out. *That was the start of our catering business, and we've never looked back since.* We started with that small birthday party, perfected our craft, and then expanded into lucrative corporate catering.

Today we only focus on catering. We no longer have our three store locations, yet we *net* more than we did when we had all of those fixed locations – with all their fixed overhead costs. Our calendar is full year-round with minimal marketing spend, time, or effort. We have a team that manages the day-to-day operations and many have been with us since the beginning.

> We didn't think of ourselves as caterers... but what a huge difference it made in our business and in our lives!

Expanding into catering has been such a blessing – getting us out of $500K in debt, getting our wonderful products into so many more mouths than we ever could have in a store, and giving us the time and financial freedom to now help you the independent coffee, smoothie, juice bar, ice cream, dessert, or snack shop owner learn how to easily snap this onto your business.

Let us share with you why, by the time you're done reading this chapter, you'll be salivating to learn more.

Gallons of Advantages

There are numerous advantages to catering:

- Advance deposits
- Limited start-up investment
- Controllable costs
- Additional revenues
- Business by contract
- Advance forecasting
- Free word-of-mouth advertising
- Selectivity

Let's discuss these items in more detail.

Advance Deposits

With catering, you can require some form of advance deposit prior to an event. This deposit provides you with some security if the event is cancelled and can also be used to purchase some or all of the supplies for the event. You'll find that many clients actually want to pay for their event ahead of time. This generates positive cash flow, and we bet you'll never complain about being pre-paid for services and having that cash in the bank.

Limited Start-up Investment

There is no need for large amounts of capital to get started. You have almost everything you need already – the commissary, the product, the staffing, and much of the equipment. It can easily cost hundreds of thousands of dollars to build out a storefront; buy equipment; and cover labor, legal, and administrative costs, etc. Plus brick-and-mortar shops require a large marketing budget to bring in new customers. These start-up and operating costs can create large cash flow challenges for the owner, struggling to sell one cup of coffee at a time to pay back the debt, many times without paying themselves anything. With catering, the largest expenditures you may have are a vehicle to do off-premise events and some mobile equipment. One catering job a month can easily cover these expenses.

Controllable Costs

Food/beverage and supply inventories, as well as operating costs, are much more easily controlled because clients must advise you in advance as to the number of guests they expect. Therefore, you only need to buy the amount necessary to serve the anticipated crowd, unlike in your shop where there could be a large variation from day to day regarding the number of patrons and menu selections. When you follow our catering system, you'll know exactly what your costs will be, and you can then price your packages accordingly to maximize profitability.

Additional Revenues

What you'll love most about off-premise catering is how easy it is to add to your existing business and the additional revenue it brings in. It's extremely profitable and offers many upsell opportunities such as additional time, alcohol service, and other accessory services. It will also bring in additional revenue to your store, as catering allows you to get your wonderful products into more people's mouths. Don't be surprised when guests at a catering job approach you and say, "Wow! This is fantastic. Where can I get this? Where is your store?" We can't tell you how many times this happened. Catering not only drives more customers to your store, it also gets you more catering jobs. People who have experienced your wonderful catering will ask you to cater *their* event. Free marketing, additional revenue. It's a wonderful – and profitable – cycle you can wash, lather, rinse, repeat.

Business by Contract

With catering, you'll have an agreement with your client laying out exactly what will be served, the timeframe, the cost, etc. This helps both sides in ensuring a successful event. Don't worry – you don't have to hire a full-time lawyer to make long, complicated contracts. We use a simple one-page agreement and have never had an issue. And yes, we've worked with large organizations that have their own in-house counsel that reviews contracts, and they even tell us how wonderfully simple our agreements are. Your clients will appreciate that you have a contract. It makes you appear professional and organized and shows that you care about the success of their event.

Advance Forecasting

With catering, events are generally booked weeks, months, or years in advance. This puts you in control of your calendar and cash flow. You'll know exactly how to staff, order product, and even when to market so that your calendar can be as full as you'd like. Wouldn't it be great to know exactly how much money you're bringing in next week, next month, or three months out? With catering, you control your calendar and your cash flow. Things slow? Go get more catering until you're at the capacity you desire.

Free Word-of-mouth Advertising

Who better to promote your catering services than the guest who just experienced it? Off-premise catering events generate tremendous amounts of free word-of-mouth advertising, which can produce future business without the necessity of advertising. One party creates future parties.

Selectivity

You also have the advantage of being somewhat selective about your clients. There are no laws that require you to accept every request to cater. If the job doesn't meet your standards, politely decline. Today, we're very selective about the catering clients we serve. We're not the most cost effective for a small birthday party, but that's not the type of catering event we like to do. Our focus is on large corporate catering jobs. Being selective allows you to maximize profits and say "no" to jobs that aren't a good fit.

Potential Drawbacks

Ready to run out and get started immediately? Awesome! There are many things to be excited about when it comes to catering, but we also want you to be aware of a few things as well:

- Seasonality
- "Stuff" happens
- Lack of a marketing system

Seasonality

Just as there are busy times in your store, you will find there are busier times with catering. Our busy season is from May through September and an extra push in December. This means you may need additional resources to take on additional jobs – vehicles, equipment, staffing, inventory, etc.

"Stuff" Happens

When you follow the Cups to Gallons model, it means you're going out to the people and providing off-premise catering. Expect "stuff" to happen. Staff that doesn't show up to work. Traffic jams that make you late. Cars that break down and/or get in accidents. Parking issues. Elevators that don't work. Equipment that breaks. Planning can help mitigate many of these but know there will be days when "stuff" hits the fan.

Lack of a Marketing System

This is the biggest reason we see people struggle when they get started. Marketing catering services is different than marketing your store. From "who" you're marketing to, the menu, the pricing, the process… if you don't have a marketing system and process in place to manage it all, you're only setting yourself up for failure. But don't worry; we're about to walk you step-by-step on how to get that marketing system in place.

There is a lot to be excited about with the catering opportunity. Ready to learn more? Now we're going to go a bit deeper and share how the Cups to Gallons model works.

Cups to Gallons, Pennies to Dollars:

- We didn't think of ourselves as caterers until a similar business suggested we could earn mid-six figures with fewer hours and more profitability.

- Advance deposits smooth out cash flow.
- Catering allows you to limit start-up expenses and continually control costs as well as providing more accurate forecasting.
- Generate additional revenue. Upselling is practically built in to catering services.
- Contracts eliminate surprises on both sides.
- Catering gets your products into more people's mouths. It's like free advertising.
- Select the clients *you* want to serve.
- While there are plenty of advantages, there can also be pitfalls. Advance planning can help mitigate them.

Grab a FREE audio recording from "Rockstar Entrepreneur" Going from $500K in Debt To A 7-Figure Profitable Business:
www.cupstogallons.com

Chapter Three:

How to Sell by the Gallon

Have you seen the price of new cars lately? It can give you sticker shock. Car dealers know this, so they change the way they present the price to you. They don't sell the car outright. They sell it as a monthly note to take away that sticker shock.

After all, would you rather pay $39,995 for a brand-new Honda Accord or lease it for only $249 a month?

Well, sticker shock applies to catering menus as well. Too many coffee, smoothie, juice bar, ice cream and dessert shops suffer from the same deadly sin: bulk pricing.

Bulk pricing is saying, "I can provide coffee for $995." Like the full car price, that sounds like a lot of money. If you divide it by the 20 guests who will be served, it comes out to almost $50 a head. Now who is going to pay that?!?!

It's one thing to *sell* by the gallon, but that doesn't mean you should *price* by the gallon. If you do, the buyer taps the recesses of their mind and thinks about what a gallon of coffee costs. If you tried to sell a gallon of coffee for $995, you'd be laughed at. You wouldn't sell one single gallon.

But we're going to show you how to get that $995 for a gallon of coffee and have your catering customers put up zero resistance to the price. In fact, they will perceive it as a bargain.

Great marketing boils down to positioning. What if we could show you how to reposition what you offer by the gallon so they don't question the price? Well, it's simple.

Just like car manufacturers have transitioned from selling based on sticker price to low monthly lease payments, you must sell your catering drinks (or ice cream, desserts, snacks, etc.) at the lowest perceived price.

An important marketing lesson to understand when it comes to selling by the gallon is: "People can buy what they *need* anywhere, but they'll pay handsomely for what they *want*."

Think about buying a car again. In general, they're all the same. They have two or four doors, four wheels, and an engine that runs it. It's just a car. It's what you need. Something to get you from point A to point B. Why then do people pay $60,000, $80,000, or even $100,000 plus for a car? Because of what they *want*. Maybe it's the "brand." Maybe it's the cup holder that lights up purple. Maybe it's the remote starter.

It's usually some little "thing," but it's the

> "People can buy what they **need** anywhere, but they'll pay handsomely for what they **want**."

thing you *want,* and when it comes down to it, it's not about price. You want that stupid little thing, and you're not leaving that dealership until you have it. That's why car dealers spend so much time showing you all of the fancy gadgets and why car companies spend so much money advertising the "experience" the car will give.

Consider Jeep®. All of their commercials show the vehicle off-roading, going up into the treacherous mountain without a problem, or driving through a river to get to the other side. Are you really going to do that every day if you buy a Jeep? Not at all likely. What you're buying (at a premium price) is what that Jeep is all about – the story, the experience, how it makes you feel. Ultimately what you're buying is what you *want.* You don't need a Jeep. You want a Jeep. And it's never about price.

Perception Over Pricing

The same holds true for what you sell. A coffee is just a coffee. A smoothie is just a smoothie. If that's what they need, they can go to any local shop and get it. Anyone can stop by Panera Bread®, pick up a box of coffee and some bagels, bring it to the office, and that's called catering. That person is not going to spend $995 for it.

However, if you sell what they *want*… to have a done-for-you solution that makes it easy for them. Something that's fun. Something that's different.

Something they can brag about. Something that makes it more than the "same ol', same ol'" stuff, they'll come to you with open wallets.

Understand this and you have the key to selling by the gallon.

Let's look at how we present our catering options:

1. First and foremost, our catering packages are based on "going to the people." Not pick-up, not delivery. There is a premium value by providing on-site service. It's all about providing an experience. When you do so, price is not the deciding factor.

2. In most cases, the person coordinating the details of the event is not an event planner, nor a caterer. They've gotten the "short stick" and are tasked with putting an event together. They are rarely making a decision solely based on price. They just want to look good (to their boss and/or their guests) and want a done-for-you solution.

3. Selling catering is all about positioning. We don't sell "smoothies" – we sell a "vacation in a cup." We don't sell "catering" – we sell "The Ultimate Hawaiian Getaway Without a 12-Hour Flight." We don't just show up and serve. We bring in a tiki bar where professional "tikitenders" blend gourmet all-natural, fresh fruit smoothies topped off

with a Hawaiian parasol. Now when you tell that to a potential catering client, do you think they care about the price? They want the *package*, the *experience*. Price is no longer a factor.

4. Of course, they'll ask for pricing. We break it down into "small pieces." A setup fee, a per person drink fee, tax, and gratuity. The client is relying on us to bring enough for everyone, and based on the number of people they tell us to serve, we know how to plan accordingly for product and staffing. Our pricing is also all-inclusive, so the client doesn't have to worry about paying extra for items such as cups, straws, napkins, etc. or running around trying to find some. We handle it all. They love that. We joke with them that they'll be the "Big Kahuna" – all they have to do is show up and get the kudos at the end for putting on such a fun and memorable event.

Cups to Gallons, Pennies to Dollars:

- It's true: You will never sell a gallon of coffee for $995.00... that causes sticker shock.
- Sell by the gallon but don't price by the gallon.

- "People can buy what they **need** anywhere, but they'll pay handsomely for what they **want**."
- Offer your clients a done-for-you experience and you'll eliminate price as a decision point.
- Offering something fun and exciting makes your client look good to their attendees with no stress or headaches on their part.
- Selling catering is all about positioning.

Want to learn more tips and strategies to go from Cups to Gallons? Join the FREE Cups To Gallons Facebook Group:
www.facebook.com/groups/CupsToGallons

Chapter Four:

Ready, Set, Cater

It never fails. During our Cups to Gallons Marketing Strategy Consultations (see Resource section), the lightbulb always goes off. Our clients are so excited to see the extra profit dollars they can make from our Cups to Gallons catering strategy. This alone often times pays for their investment in our services.

But invariably, the same question always comes up, "How do I get started?"

It's simple. You CATER... literally and figuratively.

CATER is the acronym for the five simple steps that will ramp you up from selling by the cup to selling by the gallon.

These are the same five steps we've used to transform our business from $500K in debt to a seven-figure profitable business.

These are the same five steps we teach to help other coffee, smoothie, juice bar, ice cream, and/or dessert shops implement themselves with the Cups to Gallons Training Program or with our "Done-for-You" Marketing Solutions.

These are the same five steps you can take, starting now, to stop selling by the cup and start working fewer hours and putting more money in your pocket at the end of the day.

Here's how you CATER:
        C – Change the Business Model
        A – Attention
        T – Tools and Templates
        E – Experience
        R – Ratings, Reviews and Referrals

Chapter Five:

Change the Business Model

Going out to the people is a game changer. The day you started your coffee, smoothie, juice bar, ice cream, dessert or snack shop, there was no doubt in your mind that you would be hugely successful; otherwise, you wouldn't have done it, right? Well, we have a question for you:

"Howz that workin' out for you?"

If your answer is "Not very well," you have plenty of company as that's the way most independent coffee, smoothie, juice bar, ice cream, dessert and snack shop owners answer the question.

They're working longer and harder for less money than they imagined, certainly less than they want... or need. Perhaps you can relate.

The good news is it doesn't have to be that way.

It doesn't have to be that way.

We remember sitting in our store $500K in debt wondering where our next customer was coming from. The bank was threatening to take our home. We were sued six times in one year. We scraped by, just barely able to put peanut butter and jelly on the table for our two young kids. As we'd already shared, those were very dark days.

And there was that one word that changed it all for us. That one five-letter word can change it all for you too:

CATER

Here's the thing: We had no idea what that really meant, much less how to do it. We never thought of ourselves as "caterers." We were coffee/smoothie shop owners. We were so sure people were going to bang down the door for our amazing products, stellar service, and small biz/local community vibe. Yeah, right! What we really had was a "build it and they will come" mentality.

Unfortunately, too many small business owners also have this same mentality… even when it comes to catering. Their idea of catering is someone coming in to pick up an order, like a box of coffee that person will take back to the office. Sure, that's a type of catering called pick-up catering, but pick-up catering will never take you from cups to gallons.

There's also drop-off catering, where you deliver an order but just leave it. That will never take you from cups to gallons either.

What *will* take you from cups to gallons is off-premise catering. Going out to the people, setting up and providing your service on-site, so that it's an *experience* (more on that later).

> The "C" in the CATER system is about changing the business model and taking your business to the people. **It's a game-changer.**

Whether it's a backyard party or a black-tie affair, people want a done-for-you solution. They want to work with someone who they know has great-tasting products and will do a great job. They don't want to worry about all of the details. They don't know anything about catering. They just want to be recognized and appreciated by their guests and/or employees for being the host or hostess with the "mostess." Price is rarely the deciding factor.

What makes off-premise catering the perfect solution for coffee, smoothie, juice bar, ice cream, dessert and/or snack shop owners is that it's simple. True food caterers have to bring their whole kitchen with them in order to do off-premise catering. Hot items need to remain hot (yet still taste good when served). Cold items need to remain cold (yet still taste good when served). The menu has to be carefully developed based on location, number of people, type of event, and will differ every time. Planning is critical – if you forget the main course, you're going to have a lot of hungry – and angry – people. There's a lot more investment required in equipment, supplies, and staffing. And it's a lot more competitive.

Simplicity Rules

We've been doing catering for years and we only offer four packages: smoothie bar catering, coffee bar catering, shave ice bar catering, and chocolate fountain catering. Simple. No food. All of the advantages previously mentioned. We know exactly what menu to offer, how to price it, how much product is needed, how much staffing is required. It is a true system.

Don't think you have to offer the same menu that you have in your store – you absolutely do *not* want to do that! Don't think you have to go out and become a gourmet chef and serve gourmet food. Let the food catering companies do what they do best – catering food. You do what you do best – bring your amazing coffees, smoothies, juices, ice cream, desserts and/or snacks to the people with a done-for-you model with everything made and served fresh on-site. Don't worry – we're going to teach you exactly how to do it.

When you follow the Cups to Gallons system by changing the business model and doing off-premise catering, you will differentiate yourself from every other caterer out there. And don't be surprised when food caterers call you up wanting to bring you in as part of their catering package. About 20 percent of our business is being a sub-contractor to a food caterer. They love being able to snap us on as an additional offering for their clients. The last thing they want to do is learn how to become baristas, much less buy all of the necessary equipment to do it and train their staff to do it. You can be the perfect solution for them.

We're in the Washington D.C. area, a city full of caterers. If we were to just offer pick-up or drop-off catering, we would be "just another caterer." As a "little guy," we'd have a hard time competing and getting large corporate accounts since they already have relationships with food places where they get their breakfast, lunch, and snack-type cater-in options.

Don't be one of them! Just be one. A category of one where you change the business model, go on-site, and serve your wonderful products by making it an experience. That's how you go from cups to gallons.

An added benefit of catering that most never think of is that it becomes your best marketing strategy. You're getting the opportunity to get your wonderful products into people's mouths – and you're getting paid handsomely for it!

At practically every catering job, we hear, "This tastes so amazing. Where is your store? Where can I get this? Do you have a card? I'd love to have you cater my next event." It grows upon itself and becomes a perfect trifecta:

- We get paid to do a catering job.

- We get the opportunity to get our wonderful products into more people's mouths.
- Those people love it and then come to the store and have us cater their event.

What a wonderful cycle! To think we were sitting in our store, wondering where our next customer was coming from, spending thousands of dollars on marketing to try to bring them in, and by doing one simple thing – changing the business model and going out to the people – allowed us to literally transform our business. That's why we're so passionate about helping you learn how to do the same.

It's All About Net

How would you like to make $800 for a two-hour smoothie bar catering at a graduation party, $1,600 for a shave ice bar for a corporate staff appreciation event, or $10,000 in two days for a coffee catering for a booth at a trade show? These are real-life checks we've received from off-premise catering. We *never* could make that amount of money in our store in that time frame. What's even better is that each of those catering jobs netted us between 75 – 90 percent profitability. *Yes, you read that right: 75 – 90 percent profitability.*

We have a motto, "Gross is for vanity; net is for sanity."

Net profit is what makes catering so lucrative.

Our average catering job is $800. Let's break down the numbers:

Gross revenue	$800
COGS (product)	$100
Staff cost	$100
Net profit	$600 *(75% net profitability)*

Larger events are even more profitable! Catering provides a rapid sales increase with few incremental costs.

Are you making 75 to 90 percent profitability in your store? Didn't think so. We weren't either. Despite having two stores at Dulles Airport, we were netting *more* from a few hours on a catering job than we were all day in a busy airport. We were only netting about 10 percent profit in our stores. Here's the thing: Even if we were

> Which would you prefer: 10 percent profit or 75-90 percent profit... with even fewer hours worked? Yeah, thought so.

to double sales, we wouldn't double the profitability. We'd just be selling more cups of coffee, one at a time. Which means more overhead to do so, so the net never changes much.

Catering allows you to scale, and in doing so, your profitability actually *increases*. We net more from the larger jobs than the smaller ones. That's because many times you won't serve as much as expected, so your COGS are lower, and because most jobs are for a short serving time, your staffing costs remain relatively constant.

The Cups to Gallons model is how you put more money in your bank account without a huge investment.

The good news? You already have pretty much everything you need to do this.

You have the infrastructure (your store). You have staff. You have amazing products.

You may need a few pieces of equipment – a nominal investment compared to the cost of building out your store. Ultimately, what you need is a marketing system that will have qualified leads banging down your door begging for your catering services, a process to convert them to paying clients, checklists to ensure seamless operations, providing an amazing catering experience so you get rave reviews, and clients who refer you to others, come back again and again with open wallets, and become your brand ambassadors.

Guess what? That's the rest of the CATER Marketing System. Let's dive in!

Cups to Gallons, Pennies to Dollars:

- Cater: a five-letter word that is the difference between dollars, not pennies, of profit when you change your business model.
- Cups to Gallons catering is not pick-up or drop-off catering. It's going out to the people and providing an experience.
- The beauty of the Cups to Gallons method is that it's simple and allows you to set yourself apart from your competitors... you may not even have competitors.
- Off-site catering will also drive business back to your store.
- Go from 10 percent profit to 75-90 percent profit with fewer hours worked.

Want to learn more tips and strategies to go from cups to gallons? Join the FREE Cups To Gallons Facebook Group:
www.facebook.com/groups/CupsToGallons

Chapter Six:

A ttention: Achieve Riches in Niches

Define your "who" to achieve riches in niches!

When it comes to marketing your business – whether your physical store, and especially for catering, it all comes down to one thing: getting attention.

But probably not the kind of attention you may think.

Most coffee, smoothie, juice bar, ice cream, dessert and/or snack shops think they can just put their name on a sign and run up and down the street naked saying, "Here we are; come do business with us; we do catering." Sure you'll get attention, but not the right kind of attention.

Getting attention is about defining your *"who"* ... who is your perfect customer for catering?

We talk to a lot of independent coffee, smoothie juice bar, ice cream dessert and snack shop owners, some of whom are already doing catering, but they tell us they're not happy with their results. When we ask who their perfect catering client is, we hear generic answers such as:

- Anyone within a 20-mile radius of our store
- Anyone planning a home-based party

- Anyone planning a corporate event

When you're getting started in catering, it's easy to get excited, see all the dollar signs, and think you can cater to everyone in the city you serve. That's not realistic, nor is it effective. Unless you have an unlimited marketing budget (and who does?), you'll waste time, effort and money.

That's why Stacey wrote the book, *Small Business Marketing Made EZ* that lays out the ACTION marketing system. Grab your free copy at: SmallBizMarketingSpecialist.com/book

The ACTION marketing system is a simple six-step system that you put into action – literally and figuratively – to grow a successful and profitable business. The "A" stands for attention... where it all starts.

> You can't be everything to everyone, so be something for someone.

Getting the right kind of attention means defining your "who" – who you serve. When you get this right, you'll realize there are riches in niches. By being specific in whom you serve, you'll become the go-to source for catering, differentiating yourself from your competition, and being able to charge higher prices.

To start, pick a niche on which you'd like to focus. Will it be nonprofits and associations, education and schools, military, tech, healthcare, finance, legal? Pick one that you want to start with. Then decide what type of events best match that niche. Here are different types of events that match well with coffee, smoothie, juice bar, ice cream and/or dessert catering.

In the corporate world:

- Meetings/conventions
- Incentive events
- New product introductions
- Building openings
- Recognition/staff appreciation events
- Training sessions
- Anniversaries
- Annual meetings
- Team meetings

Another niche could be individuals rather than businesses. These types of events are set up around occasions that take place in people's life cycles and include:

- Weddings
- Anniversaries
- Bar/Bat Mitzvahs
- Birthdays
- Holiday parties
- Graduations
- Births
- Reunions
- Fundraising events

As you can see, there's no shortage of the different types of catering events you can service. It's very easy to think you'll "just do them all." We were the same way when we got started. We just wanted to get as many catering jobs as possible. That's not realistic. For example, the way brides are marketed to, how they make their decisions, and what they're looking for in catering is much different than an office manager in an accounting firm looking to schedule a tax-season treat for staff or a company picnic.

What we learned the hard and expensive way is the advice we now teach our clients when it comes to getting attention: *"You can't be everything to everyone. Instead be something for someone."*

Highlight that right now! It is imperative you understand this in order to be successful in marketing your catering services. You cannot be everything to everyone. Be something for someone.

How do you become something for someone? You get crystal clear about "who" it is you serve and the unique solution you provide.

Here's how we define our "who" for corporate catering:

Carol is the HR manager at a tech company with 50 to 100 employees who was struggling to find something fun, different, and healthy to offer employees for staff appreciation events. The types of events Carol was putting together were the typical pizza parties, ice cream socials, etc. Planning and organizing them took a lot of her time (time that she couldn't *spend on her primary duties), and she rarely got any recognition for her efforts. The staff became bored of these typical events, so they rarely attended. By understanding the pain points, the goals, and a typical day for an HR manager, we were able to get her **attention** because we weren't just "selling smoothies." We were helping her become the "Big Kahuna" in the office by taking staff to Hawaii with "The Ultimate Hawaiian Getaway Without a 12-Hour Flight." Staff could come up to an authentic tiki bar where professional "tikitenders" blended gourmet, all-natural fresh fruit smoothies topped off with a Hawaiian parasol. By letting Carol know she could treat her staff to a "vacation in a cup," Carol now feels we "get" her . . . we understand her frustration in putting fun staff appreciation events together. We speak her language. We offer solutions that make her job easy and make her look great. We've got her attention. We've become "something for someone."*

As we were describing Carol, where she works, her challenges and pain in putting together staff appreciation events, did you get a clear picture in your head of "who" she is? That's exactly what you need to do. You need to be so crystal clear in whose

> With a crystal clear picture of your ideal prospect, your marketing message will be more likely to resonate and connect.

attention you're trying to get that you see that person exactly as if they're standing right in front of you.

When you get this right, your messaging will be right on target and people will feel you "get" them. It doesn't mean you can't do both weddings and corporate events. You absolutely can. It simply means that you need to know your "who" so that when you market to them, your catering packages speak specifically to what they want. The goal is to have someone feel like "Yes! This company 'gets' me and is what I'm looking for."

As you get started in catering, we suggest you start small. The residential events are great for this. They're usually 25 to 50 people, short time frames, and these are the people most likely visiting your store regularly so they're already familiar with your wonderful products and service level.

As you gain more experience, you can then go after the larger corporate-type events. The nice thing about corporate events is they're very profitable, and in most cases, once you're in, and you wow them by implementing the CATER system, they bring you back again and again. An added bonus is that as people leave their current employer and go to another company, they then bring you in to that company as well. So it grows on itself. That's the kind of marketing we like – and you will, too!

It is up to you to decide which combination of catering niches and events most appeals to you and fits best with your business objectives.

Gaining Attention

Whether you're interested in adding a new revenue stream to your existing business or just doing catering as a stand-alone business, you'll need to market your services effectively. A listing in the Yellow Pages doesn't cut it anymore. It doesn't matter how amazing your products are. "Build it and they will come" doesn't work for a store (believe us, it really doesn't!), nor does it work for catering.

To get attention, you'll need an integrated approach that combines both online and offline marketing strategies. In the next sections, we'll cover the tactics we use to market our catering services, as well as what you need to know.

Online Marketing

When people in your city need coffee, smoothie, juice bar, ice cream, dessert and/or snack catering, who do they think of?

Are you at the top of the list? The middle? Not even on it?

Chances are when someone is looking for the type of catering you offer, they're going to go to this thing called the internet to search for it. Ever heard of it? You'll want to ensure that your catering services show up in those searches and that you "look good" online – whether that's in type, images, or video and on any type/size device from something as small as a cell phone to something as large as a desktop computer monitor.

Online marketing is more than putting up a beautiful looking website, filling people's inboxes with emails, or running a bunch of random Google or Facebook ads. When it comes to online marketing, many small business owners feel like it's flushing money down the toilet because they're not seeing a positive ROI. Perhaps you can relate.

> Online marketing has so many factors that you'll need a strategy. We share ours so you can replicate it.

Don't worry. It doesn't take a huge corporate budget to compete online. We'll share exactly what we do so you can replicate it for the online marketing of your catering services.

Let's get started.

Website

Your website is the focal point for your catering marketing. It's where prospects searching for the type of catering you offer will land. The goal is to grab their attention and keep them on the page with a goal of converting them into a catering lead. The visitor coming to your catering page will, in five seconds or less, make a decision: "Should I stay or should I go?" You obviously want them to stay as long as possible. The way you do that is with a conversion-centered website design.

That conversion can be to call, fill out a "contact us" form, or send an email. What's important is to focus on a single business goal – to get a conversion. Avoid fancy design elements like flash or slide shows that slow down your site and do nothing to convert.

You want a site that has a professional-looking design that's easy to navigate, displays your services, and is mobile responsive (meaning people can view it on a phone or tablet). Not sure if yours is? Input your URL at https://responsivedesignchecker.com/ to see how your website looks on every size device.

Here are three things you *don't* want to include on your catering page(s):

- **Your pricing** – When you follow the CATER system, people will not be basing their decision on price. If you put your pricing on your website, you've made yourself a commodity, and prospects who happen to come upon your site and think, "Hmmm... this sounds expensive. I'm going to shop around" will leave and most likely never return. You want that prospect to contact you, so you can "sell" the catering experience you provide and make it appear you're customizing the package specifically to that prospect. (We'll share exactly how we do this when we cover the "T" in the CATER system.)

- **The ability to order online** – For the same reasons we just noted about pricing, you should not allow anyone to order off-premise catering via your website. What if three people ordered catering for the same day and time, and you weren't able to accommodate? What if it's a job you're not interested in doing? What if the customer orders incorrectly, and they think the pricing is one amount but it ends up being different? Then you're just making your customer angry. We've found that with catering, people want a more personal relationship. They have questions. They have concerns. They want to ensure their event will be a huge success. Make it clear in your website copy that every event is different, so you want them to contact you to discuss how you can make their unique event special.

- **"I I I" or "We We We" speak** – Look at your "About Us" page and count how many I's or We's are on the page. It's like George of the Jungle beating his chest so proud that he could just ramble on forever. Here's the truth: the last thing catering prospects care about is you. They don't care that you say you have the best service. They don't care that you say you have the best products. They don't care that you've been in business since 1492. They only care about one thing: themselves! Make sure your copy talks to their needs, their wants, their goals.

Now that you know what *not* to have on your website, here's what you *DO* want to include:

- **Professional images** – Hire a professional to do a photo shoot (don't use stock photos) and have a gallery that shows recent catering events. We see too many websites all focused on "product" – images of the food/drink. Your visitor wants to understand what the catering experience is all about, and that's the people part of it. Show pictures of happy people enjoying their food/drink and consider adding video.
- **Include video** – The power of video today cannot be denied. Videos are easy to watch on any type of device, and they have a visual appeal that static content simply can't match. When we see a customer truly enjoying their beverage or a host that is thrilled with their service, we ask if we can take a quick testimonial video. Most are agreeable.

Want to see our catering services page? Visit: https://mauiwowidc.com/catering

- **Social proof** – It doesn't matter what you say about yourself that matters; it's what others say about you that matters. Show any awards you've won, raving reviews, and testimonials on your site. Our favorite way to show social proof is to feature the logos of companies for which we've done catering events. We had a company call us and say, "I saw you did an event at Chadbourne. They're our competition. If they're using you and had an amazing experience, we want to use you also."

- **Guarantee** – Allay any concerns catering prospects may have by offering a guarantee. Don't worry – if you follow the CATER system, your clients will be thrilled. We've never had anyone ask for their money back per the guarantee.

Search Marketing

Most of your new catering clients will find you via online search, so being visible is vital to your marketing.

There are two types of search marketing:

- Pay-per-click (PPC). You bid for position on the page and pay each time someone clicks through to your website. These are the ads or sponsored listings that show up on the top and/or bottom of the search result pages.

- Search-engine-optimization (SEO). This is organic search, which is free, but it's based on how Google views the relevancy of your content as it relates to the search. There are only a few organic search spots on page one, so it takes time and also requires that you add fresh content to your website regularly.

You'll also want to make sure you have a Google My Business page set up. This is Google's "local marketing" platform for geo-targeted searches showing a map and customer reviews. Google wants to ensure that users searching for something get the best/most pertinent search results. With catering, Google understands that someone searching for that is most likely looking for a local option, so if you're searching for the service in California, Google is not going to show you caterers in Minnesota. That's where Google My Business helps. An added bonus is the ability to optimize your page with keyword-rich descriptions and by getting customer reviews. Google features

> Be certain to set up your Google My Business page!

companies that have the highest ratings – because they want the user to have a good experience using their site. It's critical that you work hard to get excellent reviews and ratings posted online (more on that to come).

If you optimize all of these channels, you can show up in the three places on page one of search:

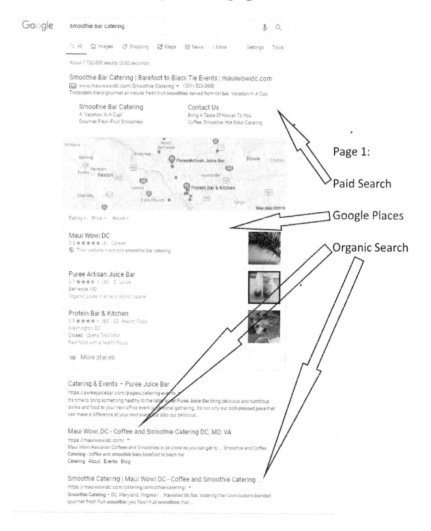

Note that the top slot is an ad. That's "pay to play." We have the top slot because we pay to be there, but we also have the most relevant content related to the search term "smoothie bar catering."

Next is Google Places, showing where we are on the map and our reviews. We have the top slot because we have great reviews and content specific to the search term.

The two organic listings feature keyword-rich content on our website.

When someone searches for "smoothie bar catering," we dominate the first page, and that's because we know how to optimize online search to our advantage. It's a combination of "pay to play," "local marketing/reputation management," and "content marketing."

PPC can be very expensive, especially for a generic term like "catering." Terms like coffee catering and smoothie catering range from $6 to $10/click. That's for one click. So if someone clicks that ad, goes to our catering page and then leaves (bounces) without contacting us, that's $6 to $10 down the drain. You can see how quickly that can add up and potentially flush money down the toilet with online advertising. But we know our numbers. An average catering job is $800, so would we pay $6 - $10 to have someone click our ad to learn more about our catering services? Yes!

We monitor our ad spend and build the plan around peak seasons. For example, when spring rolls around, we up our ad spend for smoothie catering. At the same time, we decrease our ad spend for hot chocolate catering. In the winter months, we do the opposite. We up our ad spend for coffee and hot chocolate catering and decrease it for smoothies and shave ice.

To help maximize your organic ranking for searches, set up a blog and post helpful content consistently. Your blog can cover a lot of ground including telling the story of your catering business, answering questions, revealing "how-to" recipes, talking about recent events, and more.

Not only is your blog the perfect venue for you to add fresh content to your site (which helps SEO), but it also shows your customers that you're an authority in your field. Every time you add another blog post, you give both search engines and readers another reason to check out your website, and both of those factors can make your website stronger.

Social Media Marketing

Social media platforms such as Facebook, Twitter, Instagram, LinkedIn, and Alignable create fantastic opportunities to promote your catering services, show via pictures and video what you do, generate excitement, offer promotions, tag clients, post reviews, and more. You can also consider setting up a few boards on Pinterest, themed around the different niches your catering business serves, such as weddings, family reunions, or holiday parties.

It's important to train staff to take pictures at every catering event and send those to you. One, it allows you to see the setup and ensure that everything is correct. There have been a few occasions when staff sent us pictures from an event where the setup needed to be modified because it was incorrect. Two, you can then use those pictures for social media, to send to the client after the event (many hostesses are so busy they don't have time and/or forget to take pictures, so they're so grateful when you do this), and to add to your website gallery.

You'll want to build out a content calendar, so you can ensure you're posting well enough in advance of holidays and/or peak seasons. For example, when

> Create a content calendar so your social media posts are relevant and coherent.

spring rolls around if you're focusing on the wedding market, you'll want to make sure you have social media content focused on that already in place. Note holidays that could be a "reason why" to have catering such as July 4th, Christmas, end-of-tax season, summer picnics, etc.

Remember that a great deal of marketing success has to do with timing. Be visible with your best content and offers when the iron is hot. If you have a physical store, you'll want to balance your catering posts with in-store promotions.

When it comes to managing your social media accounts, you'll need to decide how that will be handled. Will you do it? Will a staff person be responsible for it? Should you use a social media management company?

There's pros and cons to each. Spending your time on social media is probably not the best use of your time, especially if there are multiple platforms to manage. However, if you're just starting out, it can be a good way to learn more about it and understand what types of posts resonate best on each platform. Having a staff person manage your social media means that they'll have to find the time on a daily basis to plan out a content calendar, schedule posts, engage with people, build a following, and respond to messages. It usually also requires some graphic design and/or picture/video editing expertise.

Balancing the workload of social media with everything else on a day-to-day basis can be challenging. The last thing you want to do is to have a piece-meal approach to your social media. Therefore, consider hiring an outside company to manage it for you. They'll understand the nuances of each social platform and how to optimize it for search and engagement. They'll also understand the insights and metrics into what's working and what's not. And they should have the graphic design expertise needed to ensure what's being posted is maximized for engagement and shareability. Yes, we can help – happy to chat with you about it.

Because of the variety of social media sites and their corresponding paid ad opportunities (e.g., Facebook and LinkedIn ads), and the fact that they often update and change, we'd be happy to discuss the options and perhaps determine the best place for you to start. Grab a slot on our calendar: https://calendly.com/smallbizstacey/cups-to-gallons-free-consult

Email Marketing

What do you check first thing when you wake up – social media or email? Most people check both of these continually throughout the day. Email is a great marketing tool to stay in touch with prospects, clients, and past clients. It's an inexpensive tool that generates new business, repeat business, and sets you apart from the competition.

While it seems simple (just collect email addresses and hit send, right?), it's important to know how to do it correctly; otherwise, you very likely will end up in the spam folder, people will unsubscribe, or even worse, refuse to do business with you.

There are many email marketing tools on the market today. You can set up a free account with MailChimp that allows you to email up to 2,000 contacts (as of this publishing), tag and segment your lists, and set up basic templates. It's very user-friendly and has other monthly packages available from which to choose. We used Constant Contact for many years as our email marketing platform. It's a bit more expensive than MailChimp, but it has a lot of features and is very easy to use. Pricing is based on your list size.

Today, we use a CRM (customer relationship management) tool called Infusionsoft by Keap. It is a comprehensive automated platform that manages our entire catering process from a lead coming in to past clients returning. Ultimately, it allows us to deliver the right message to the right person at the right time. In addition, it also shows us exactly how much money we're going to make today, tomorrow, and next month based on what's in our pipeline. If you're just getting started, we suggest using a more basic email marketing tool such as MailChimp or Constant Contact. Clients who have us provide done-for-you marketing services get all of

> Don't send the same email to everyone... unless you don't care if no one reads it!

the benefits of Infusionsoft to manage their entire process. Feel free to reach out to us if you want more information.

We could write an entire book on email marketing but here are our top tips:

- **Segment and personalize your catering emails.** Would you be more likely to open an email that was specific to you, your interests and your needs, or a plain vanilla generic email that was obviously sent to everyone? Segmentation gives you the ability to write more targeted content that people want to read, thus improving your open rates and ultimately getting more people to contact you wanting to learn more. We segment our emails by the type of catering in which they're interested (smoothie, coffee, shave ice, hot chocolate) as well as by the type of event (wedding, corporate, residential). This allows us to send specific messages and offers that resonate with the reader. That's why our open and click-through rates are well above the industry average. Whenever we want our phone to ring, we send out an email. It works every single time.

- **Send timely content they want to read.** Most people think that sending timely content means sending a "Happy Holidays" email to all of your contacts once a year. You and I both know that you can do better. Identify trends in the niche(s) on which you've chosen to focus your catering efforts. For example, if wedding season is coming up, you can use this knowledge to ramp up your emails that are targeted toward brides-to-be or wedding planning businesses and stay ahead of the curve with your marketing. Another way to be timely with your email marketing is to remind clients to do business with you again. We send, "It's Been A Year" emails to clients that remind them how much they loved the service and to contact us to ensure they can get on our calendar.

- **Craft click-worthy subject lines**. Your goal is to pique your readers' curiosity so they want to read more. Some of our best performing headlines are:
    o *"Can't get enough of this"*
    o *"Pssst . . . New Fall Beverage Treats for Your Next Event"*
    o *"Did someone say tiki bar?????"*
    o We've had great success in using emojis in headlines as well
- **Personalize your messaging.** This is more than just inserting someone's name into the email. Everyone you email is unique. They will likely only respond to messages that resonate with them. You do this by segmenting your list according to demographics (e.g., gender, age, educational level, etc.) and/or purchasing

behaviors (e.g., coffee catering, smoothie catering, etc.). As an example, we send targeted emails to accounting firms during tax season promoting a tax-season break/treat. If we were to send that same message to law firms, it wouldn't make any sense. We have different emails that go out to different segments, so we're always "delivering the right message to the right person at the right time."

- **Send emails regularly.** You may find that surprising, but by showing up in the inbox on a regular basis makes them remember you. That's especially true if your emails come packed with tons of value. Remember: Every email you send doesn't have to – and shouldn't – just sell, sell, sell. When you publish a new blog, send out an email. When you have a new beverage, product, or catering service, send out an email. Let customers get to know your staff. Have a regular e-newsletter to stay front-of-mind and share pictures and testimonials from past events. You can also obviously tie your email marketing initiatives in with what you're doing to market your brick-and-mortar store.

Email marketing has many benefits. It's cost effective compared to other marketing channels. The availability of analytics tools lets you know what's working so you can build better emails each time. And you save trees, too. But as you'll see later on in offline marketing, we're big proponents of direct mail as well.

Video

The power of video today cannot be denied. Videos are easy to watch on any type of device, and they have a visual appeal that static content just can't match.

Videos are particularly powerful for catering because it allows people to see what your experience is all about.

You can use video to show your staff serving at an event, testimonials, even live from the event if your client allows.

Tip: Post your videos on your website and optimize for searches on YouTube.

Blogging and the Media

You don't have to be a journalist to provide people with useful information. Blog about the local scene, about your recipes, about events you've participated in – or will be participating in, and of course, about events you've catered. Provide helpful advice to those who are planning events or looking for advice. Posting regularly to your blog will help others view you as the local authority and someone they trust.

Most caterers aren't leveraging their greatest potential asset when it comes to marketing: the army of content-starved local news and food and event bloggers out there who will publish compelling marketing content about you.

Target local media and nurture these relationships. Reach out and ask if you can contribute a guest post on their blog for a link back to your catering website. A caterer who specializes in cakes could target wedding or event bloggers and media contacts. Or you could offer to write a post about fun staff appreciation catering ideas for a local human resources association.

Start by researching what sites and/or media are in your area that provide the opportunity to gain exposure for your catering services. Most blogs include contact information or a "How to Work with Us" page somewhere on their site. Google local food writers in your area. Use LinkedIn to research and connect with these media sources. Offer a free tasting, so they may write about you. Food writers often have social media networks of their own. Their mentions could drive new catering business your way.

Offline Marketing

All the hype you hear about search marketing, social media, and websites can leave you thinking all you need is to build your online presence and let the leads come rolling in.

Make no mistake about it. Online marketing is powerful. It will get you attention. It will be a big lead generator.

But don't sit on your laurels. The rules of online marketing change daily, and you don't want to wake up one day only to find out that Google or Facebook changed something in their algorithm that impacts how you are found online. Never put all of your marketing eggs into one basket. We always advise our clients to implement an integrated marketing approach that is a combination of both online and offline marketing strategies. Let's review the offline marketing strategies you'll want to implement to get attention for your catering services.

Word-of-Mouth Buzz and Referrals

The best possible potential catering customers are the ones you already have: the guests at your catering events. There's no better way to show people what your catering services are all about than to have them experience it first-hand. Photos and website copy alone don't allow someone to taste your amazing products and don't show the amazing customer service you provide.

> Combine online and offline marketing for the greatest impact and success.

While you don't want to overtly or aggressively promote your catering services while on a catering job, you can put a small stack of business cards and/or flyers on the bar for people to pick up. It's a subtle way of advertising your services to guests who are already familiar with the quality of your work as it's happening in real time.

Don't be surprised if people approach you directly and ask you about catering their event. Make sure you get their contact information so you can follow up. We have forms we send with our catering staff that they can use to obtain this information. We also incentivize our staff with a $25 bonus for any referred catering job they bring us. What gets rewarded gets done, and it is rare to not get at least one new referral from every catering job we do.

The best time to ask for a referral is when your client is thrilled with the service provided. However, we suggest not running up to them right after the event asking, "You loved it? Great. Who do you know who would love it also?" That can come across very negatively and creepy. Let your client bask in the accolades they get from their guests and send a follow-up afterward to get a rating, review, and referral. (More on this when we cover the "R" in the CATER system.)

Four-Walls Marketing

If you have a brick-and-mortar location, then you definitely want to implement four-walls marketing: your store.

Your loyal store customers are the best tool you have to get the word out. They already know you, like you, and trust you. If I come in and get my daily cup of coffee from you or bring my family in on Saturday or Sunday morning, obviously I like your beverages, food, and service. You don't have to sell me on doing business with you. A lot of your customers are happy to buy other things from you when they realize that you offer them. Four-walls marketing means using your four walls to get the word out about your catering. That involves all kinds of different tools. We're going to run through a variety of them:

Table Tents

When someone visits your store, you have a captive audience. If they're taking their beverage to-go, they're usually waiting in an area with condiments and additional items they may want for their beverage. Why not have signage and/or brochures in this area promoting your catering services? The person having their beverage in the store will be sitting at a table or a bar, and with table signage, they can easily see that you offer catering. That might prompt them to think about an event they have coming up that needs catering.

Signs

You could put a sign in your lobby, on windows/walls, or on the outside of your building. Banners are another four-walls marketing tool you can use if you have the space on your building to mount one.

Our favorite four-walls marketing tool is the washroom sign. These are signs you can put up over urinals and mount to the bathroom stall doors.

You always have a captive audience in the bathroom. They're not going anywhere. While they're taking care of business, they can read about your business. This is an incredible tool to promote catering.

Flyers

Have flyers on your counter that customers can pick up and look at while they're waiting for their order. You can also attach them to every takeout order. Most restaurants are doing five or ten percent of their sales in takeout, so why not attach a catering flyer to every order?

Buttons

Have your servers and front-line team wear buttons promoting your catering services. As a general rule, most front-line staff people are not going to promote catering, but anyone can wear a button that says, "Bring Our Shop to You – Ask Me How!" Once they're asked what the button means, they can talk about your catering program. It's a great way to get the word out about catering.

We have many clients who are using our catering giveaway signs. Let's say you're giving away a free catering for ten. Instead of a fish bowl giveaway that you drop business cards in, I recommend having your customers fill out a qualifying questionnaire. Have them include both personal and work contact information as well as information that's relevant. Have them fill out who is in charge of catering at their company, how often they bring in catering, and how many people they get catering for. By qualifying the prospects, you now have entry into businesses where some of your customers work

Pimp Your Catering Ride

When you follow the Cups to Gallons model, you're taking your catering services to the people. That means you need a vehicle. You're going to be on the road, so why not make that vehicle eye-catching with a wrap?

We wrap all of our vehicles, and it is marketing that pays for itself multiple times over. Our trucks are bright and vibrant – so much so that we joke that we think we cause a lot of accidents as we always see people pointing and taking pictures of it. We've had people call us from the road noting they saw the truck, so we know it works.

To leverage it further, we add business card holders to each side of the truck. It's an easy way for people to get your contact information. These work so well that we have to fill them about once a week.

Networking

You're a small local business. Leverage that. Connecting with people is the key to your success. Network with event and wedding planners, golf clubs, sports clubs, etc. Remember how you defined your "who"? What types of businesses can connect you with that person or business? That's who you want to network with.

Get involved in your local community. Join the local Chamber of Commerce. Get involved in your church, PTA meetings, neighborhood events. Always have business cards on you, especially a digital business card.

The key to making networking successful is to not be a wallflower. That won't work. You have to get out there, speak to people, and tell them what you have to offer. When speaking with people, put their needs and interests first. See how you can help them. No one wants the first thing they hear from you to be, "Hey baby, wanna buy my stuff?" aka "know anyone who needs my catering services?" That's creepy and annoying. Be a true go-giver. Listen more than you speak. Ask questions to understand what the person does, what their challenges are, and how you can help.

Consider offering a referral bonus to partners who refer business to you. We offer ten percent of every catering job to the referrer. Some use it as a discount on their services. Some prefer to receive a check.

What happens when someone asks for your business card? They put it "away" and ultimately end up forgetting about it. Or it gets stuck in a pile with a bunch of other business cards never to be found again – meaning they won't contact you. And chances are, you do the same when someone hands you their business card.

> A digital business card also gets you valuable contact information!

We love the power of a digital business card. It's nothing more than your business card as a photo on your phone. When someone asks for your business card, tell them you have a digital business card. They'll be intrigued and ask about it. Tell them you'll text it to them. Do it right then and there. Guess what? You just got their phone number and can now follow up with them at a later date. They now also have your card in their phone, so the next time someone mentions that they're looking for catering, they'll remember speaking with you and can then share that digital business card quickly and easily with others.

You should have printed business cards as well. We print on both sides of the card – why not? You've got the real estate, use it. We put our contact information on the front and our core catering services on the back. The card is colorful and attractive, so people want to keep it. We use thick quality card stock, so the cards don't get torn easily. We always have printed business cards at every catering job. There is rarely an event where someone doesn't ask for one.

Join Catering Associations

Beyond just local networking, consider joining professional associations such as the National Association of Catering Executives. Here you can get more information on the catering profession, industry trends, marketing tips, vendor information and make important connections within the industry.

We joined our local chapter, and it was a great opportunity to connect with caterers, meeting and event planners, and even set up our coffee and smoothie bars at educational and networking events, so members could taste and experience what our catering services were like. This way it's easy for them to make a decision when bringing us in as a sub-contractor since they know exactly what they're getting.

Get Placement on "Preferred Vendor" Venue Lists

Most major venues available for rental, including banquet halls, event spaces, or even private outdoor venues maintain some sort of "preferred vendor" list that they hand to their customers who may be booking the space or looking for catering services. Some event spaces may even require their customers to choose a caterer from their preferred list, which means it's definitely a list on which you want to have your business name included.

Work a Few Morning Farmer's Markets

This is different from town to town, but many farmer's markets have dramatically underserved options, especially when it comes to gourmet coffee, smoothies, juices, ice cream, desserts and/or snacks. Setting up a booth and giving out samples of your best menu items, and selling them in full size, is a great way to introduce people in your community to the quality of your food/beverages and to promote your store and catering services, while rubbing elbows with potential customers. These customers go to these farmer's markets because they support the small businesses in their community. Of course, you'll want to populate your booth with plenty of business cards, flyers, and take-away marketing materials for all of the new contacts you've made.

Treat Local Businesses to Samples

This is a great option if your city or town has a condensed "Main Street" area lined with local businesses. This also works well in larger industrial and/or business parks. Take an afternoon to hit the streets, offering samples of your catering wares to offices and local businesses. No one complains when free food/drink arrives. Many small businesses are looking for what you offer as something fun and different for their meetings and staff appreciation events. Remember to focus your attention and charm on whomever is working at the front desk; they're many times the ones who order food and book caterers, not the CEOs. And if they're not, they can point you in the right direction to who handles it – usually an office and/or HR manager.

Seek Partnerships with Complementary Businesses

If you're focusing on catering weddings or receptions, find a florist that will recommend your services, add you to their vendor list, or even allow you to place marketing materials in their store. If you're looking to do more of the "birthday and reunion" type events, approach your local party rental store about a potential partnership. Most small businesses are happy to help complementary services get their foot in the door, particularly if your services don't directly compete with their own.

Our favorite place to research and connect with these partnership opportunities is Alignable. This social media platform is the perfect place for you to focus on building relationships with other local businesses. You can post and share your catering packages as a service on your business profile and that gets shared to everyone in your network.

Reason Why Marketing

"Reason why" marketing is giving people a reason to do business with you. Let's say it's the New Year – many companies have kick-off and planning meetings. That's a *reason why* they would want to bring you in to cater. You could market a gourmet coffee bar to "caffeinate" everyone and get them "charged up" for the new year.

Here are other times of the year you can easily use in creating a "reason why" someone would want to have you cater their event:

- **Tax Season** – Staff is working long, hard hours and the company wants to recognize and appreciate their efforts.
- **Valentine's Day** – Everyone wants to do something "sweet" that's fun and memorable. What's better for that than your catering packages?
- **Summer Cool Down** – When it's blistering hot outside, having something cool and refreshing, whether it's for a birthday party, company picnic, pool party or any outdoor event, you can be the "cool" treat.
- **Christmas/Holiday Season** – It's the season of eating and drinking; your catering packages can be the perfect solution.

These are obvious reasons why someone may be interested in catering. Our favorite reason why marketing strategy is to tap into the many fun, unique, and many times quirky holidays that could tie into what you offer.

Did you know there's:
- National Popcorn Day (January 19)
- National Cherry Month (February)
- National Donut Day (June 7)
- Walk on Your Wild Side Day (April 12)
- Do Something Nice Day (October 5)

Of course, there are the major holidays everyone knows about – President's Day, July 4th, Thanksgiving, etc. Those are easy "reason why" holidays you can use to offer catering services.

Our favorite site to find holidays we want to tap into is holidayinsights.com. There are "monthly" holidays, food holidays, just-for-fun holidays, and more. We love to pick a fun quirky holiday and tie our catering packages into that. For example, if we see that August 22nd is "Eat A Peach Day," we could promote peach smoothie catering packages. It's a "reason why" someone could have us come in and do catering.

Sometimes we leverage the food holidays and offer it as a "bonus" for booking us. For example, we've offered free popcorn as part of our packages during the week of National Popcorn Day. It's a simple snap-on and gives people a reason why to bring us to their event. Or National Chocolate Chip Cookie Day.

We offer free chocolate chip cookies when a client books a coffee catering job on that day.

Pick one holiday each month you'd like to use for your "reason why" marketing. You can then build your marketing campaigns ahead of time and have them ready to go in various formats – four-walls marketing, email marketing, social media, direct mail, even on your website. Your customers will love the different campaigns you come up with and will look forward to see what the next "theme" will be, so they can have a reason why to have you cater.

Print Newsletters

Sure it's easy and low-cost to send out an electronic newsletter, but sending print newsletters is the most effective way to increase retention rates, increase referrals, and instantly build long-lasting relationships with your customers.

Retention

A monthly print newsletter allows your clients to feel like they're being kept in the loop — which means they'll be less likely to leave your inner circle when the competition comes a-calling. Plus, customers who stick around for the long haul are more likely to spend more money within your business. In fact, it's more than 50 percent easier to sell new products or services to your existing clients than it is to a new lead or prospect — and just a five percent bump in retention could result in as much as a 25 percent increase in profitability. When you consider that 80 percent of your future revenue will likely come from just 20 percent of your existing clients... well, retention rates suddenly seem pretty important.

Referrals

Sending a regular print newsletter is a surefire way to stay "top of mind," and your clients are more likely to pass along a name they actually remember (hint: yours). On top of that, because a print newsletter is a physical object, it can easily be picked up and passed around — which is exactly what your clients are going to do with it. When you send out a monthly print newsletter, you're automatically reaching new customers way beyond your mailing list.

Relationships

The number one reason to send out a print newsletter is simply this: to build relationships. After all, people like to work with people they know and like, and what's the easiest way for your clients to get to know you? You got it - a custom newsletter. A newsletter can transform you from a nameless, faceless catering business to a "friend" your clients know and enjoy interacting with. Suddenly, their willingness to trust you increases tenfold — and their loyalty along with it. Now that's the power of relationships.

Direct Mail

Independent coffee, smoothie, juice bar, ice cream, dessert and snack shop owners reach out to us and say, "There's so many marketing strategies we can implement to get catering jobs. Which is the best? What worked best for you?"

Our answer is always the same: direct mail. If we could only have one marketing strategy to promote our catering services, this is the one we'd hold near and dear.

Direct mail is very broad and can include postcards, letters, self-mailers, and "lumpy mail."

Our most successful direct mail piece is a form of "lumpy mail." We call it a "smoothie-in-a-box." What is lumpy mail?

Lumpy mail is like it sounds. A piece of mail that is "lumpy," meaning it has bulk to it. It's something that gets the person to stop and want to open it to know what's inside.

> We could write a whole book on all of the different types of direct mail with examples of each. Maybe that will be our next one. ☺

We've mailed letters that included sunglasses, flip flops, even chap stick. But the one piece that always outperforms all of those is our smoothie-in-a-box package. It's such a successful marketing piece, it's like printing money. Everytime we send them out, money flows in.

The inside is what really makes it work and we share every secret detail in our Cups to Gallons Training Program.

Here are the hard facts of this mailer:

- It costs about $5.00 to send including postage (which is just a little over $2.00/box).
- Our average catering job is $800.
- For every three boxes we send out, two become paying catering clients.

Would you spend $5 to make $800? How about spending $15 to make $1,600? Yeah, wash, lather, rinse, repeat. And that's what we do. When our calendar is slowing down, we send out a few smoothie-in-a-box packages and voila! The calendar quickly fills up again. This direct mail piece is so successful we've actually had to stop sending them out because our calendar is now full year-round, but the few times we notice it's starting to slow down, we just send out a few of these boxes.

You now know how to get attention. First define your "who," then build out the marketing strategies you'll use to reach those people to make them aware of your catering services. Don't feel like you have to do all of these within the first week. It's not realistic you'll be able to, and you'll end up frustrated with the results.

Start with one online and one offline marketing strategy. Get the systems in place, so the marketing runs on autopilot. Speaking of systems... on to the next chapter.

Cups to Gallons, Pennies to Dollars:

- Clearly define your "who," and remember there's riches in niches.
- You can't be everything to everyone. Instead be something for someone.
- Ensure your website converts; include what it should have and exclude what shouldn't be there.
- Determine if you want to pursue PPC, but be certain you set up your Google My Business page.
- Social media is a driving force, but it's time consuming. Do it well or ask for help with it.
- Email marketing can be a huge, cost-effective marketing approach, but you can't send the same message to everyone or you're wasting time.
- Don't overlook videos and blogging!
- Your best catering prospect are your current customers. Get referrals.

- Use the four walls in your store and table tops to promote your catering service. Ditto to your vehicle.
- Network, join associations, get on preferred vendor lists, and share samples in your community.
- There's no shortage of "reasons why" someone would want you to cater their event. Get creative.
- Print newsletters and direct mail still rock.

When it comes to getting attention and building out your marketing plan, it can seem very overwhelming. Grab a free copy of Stacey's book Small Business Marketing Made EZ to get the six simple steps you can use to get your marketing into ACTION:

https://SmallBizMarketingSpecialist.com/book

Chapter Seven:

Tools & Templates

Catering: it's all about systems.

Some people have nightmares about showing up at work naked. Coffee caterers have nightmares about showing up to an event without espresso beans.

You probably have systems in place in your shop. Systems so that your wonderful food and beverages are made the same way every time. Systems so that employees know their schedules. Systems so that from the time you open until the time you close, everyone knows what to do and how to do it. Wash, lather, rinse, repeat.

In order to make your catering business hugely successful and profitable, you also need a system. That's why the "T" in the CATER system is so important – tools and templates to ensure a seamless process from beginning to end.

We won't be able to go in-depth on all of the tools and templates you'll need to do off-premise catering here in this book because of space limitations. The Cups to Gallons Catering Training Program covers it all. Choose from either a two-day live event training experience or invest in the online program with over 20 hours of in-depth training on every aspect of getting your Cups to Gallons catering program going.

But we'll certainly give you a taste, and what we'll cover here is:

- Crafting the perfect menu
- Sales scripting and managing catering relationships from inquiry to returning client
- Equipment

But First...

Where do you start when it comes to getting into catering? There are two very important, unsexy, things you'll want to make sure you do first – understand health department and insurance requirements. Let's get those out of the way now.

We're not attorneys and we don't play one on TV. However, we do want you to be structured for success in getting started with catering and have the right tools and templates in place. What we share below is *our* experience in running our catering business. Every locality is different and the laws vary, so *please* do your homework, check with any appropriate agencies, and ask your attorney for advice.

A common question we're asked is, "Do I need a special license or certification to do catering?" In general, "No." You do not have to get a license and/or permit for each catering job. However, you must operate in compliance with your municipality's food code and other ordinances.

A food and/or beverage establishment doing catering is responsible for maintaining control of and ensuring the safety of the food/beverage from preparation to service to the consumer. Protect food/beverage during storage, preparation, transportation, and serving to prevent cross-contamination and contamination by dust, insects, or other sources. Keep equipment and vehicles clean.

When food is prepared for a catering event, the following five factors can increase the risk of a foodborne illness outbreak:

- Poor employee health and hygiene
- Improper cooking temperatures and times
- Food from unsafe sources
- Improper hot and cold holding temperatures and times
- Cross-contamination and contaminated equipment

Five effective control measures to reduce the risk of a foodborne illness outbreak are:

- Exclude ill employees, wash hands properly, and prevent bare-hand contact with ready-to-eat food.
- Cook raw animal foods to the temperatures and times required according to your state code.
- Verify that all food is from approved sources, received at required temperatures, and in good condition.

- Keep food out of the temperature danger zone (between 41°F and 135°F).
- Properly store food, and wash, rinse, and sanitize food-contact surfaces.

Caterers must meet safe operation requirements including water supply, sewage disposal, and utilities.

Each catering business is unique, and operators should discuss menu and food flow, volume and timing, equipment, cleaning and sanitizing, and utilities with their inspector or appropriate agency to determine specific requirements.

Insurance Considerations

You would never open up your shop without the appropriate insurance in place. Make sure you have adequate coverage for catering as well.

After all, you will be handling and serving food/drinks, and your employees will be in vehicles headed to each catering job. There are three main categories of insurance you'll need to consider:

- General liability
- Liquor liability
- Auto coverage

Let's go a bit deeper on each type:

General Liability

If you're in business, you need general liability insurance – no ifs, ands, or buts about it.

When it comes to business insurance, this is the baseline and first type of policy you should purchase. It gives you peace of mind knowing that, in the case of an accident or other catastrophe, your business is protected.

A few years ago, there was a derecho in our city on July 3rd. For us, July 4th is one of our busiest days of the year. We had large tiki bars already set up on a pier at National Harbor, and we were contracted for multiple events that day. Well, when we woke up, trees were strewn all over the place (it was like a tornado came through). We could not get out of the neighborhood. There was no power... for 10 days.

> Liability insurance is a must for every business!

When we were finally able to get out of the neighborhood and check on equipment already placed at events, we saw one of our tiki bars completely ruined and one was hanging over the edge of the pier. Our trailer had a gaping hole in it (obviously something slammed into it). Without power for 10 days, all of our smoothie mix went bad. And we lost thousands of dollars of revenue from not being able to do the jobs.

It could have put us out of business. But we had general liability insurance. Our insurance company sent a rep out immediately to assess the damage, and they cut us an initial check right on the spot. Because we had the right coverage in place, we were reimbursed for everything – equipment, product loss, and even lost revenue.

Like most insurance plans, your policy will clearly outline its limit, or the maximum amount the insurance company will pay against a liability claim. It's important to assess your risk carefully to ensure you have adequate coverage and won't be left paying for expenses out of pocket.

Most general liability insurance policies cover up to one million per occurrence and two million in aggregate; if you need additional coverage, it is common to double the limits. If you need more than two million per occurrence, you most likely have to purchase an umbrella or excess insurance policy.

For example, if your business is sued for $300,000 in medical costs associated with a slip-and-fall injury, but your policy limit is $250,000, you will have to cover the difference of $50,000 yourself. It is important to speak to an insurance agent to understand what is – and isn't – covered before investing in a policy. And let them know you'll be doing off-premise catering, so they can add the correct riders (if necessary) based on your needs.

Insurance is one of those things you hate paying every month until *wham* – "something happens" – and then you realize how grateful you are that you had it. We sure were!

Protect yourself, protect your business, and ensure you have the right coverage in place for your needs.

With catering, you will find that many companies, especially if they're in a larger building run by a property management company, will require a COI (certificate of insurance). Make sure the insurance company you work with will provide these for you and whether there's any cost associated with it. (We get unlimited free COI requests with our insurance provider.)

Liquor Liability Insurance

You will be asked if you can serve alcohol in your drinks. For most people, alcohol = celebration. Whether it's a birthday party, holiday event, graduation party, even a corporate event, if your business serves alcohol, you could be at risk. A single claim could ruin the business you've worked hard to build.

Liquor liability insurance protects caterers against lawsuits, legal claims, and damages stemming from the service of beer, wine, or liquor. Examples of claims related to liquor liability are:

- Property damage caused by an intoxicated guest
- Accidents involving someone who was served alcohol by your staff
- You serve too much alcohol to someone who injures themselves as a result

We have a rider on our policy that covers our staff serving alcohol. We call it a "license to pour." We do not buy nor provide any alcohol. The client must provide it. Any of our staff who serve alcohol must be TIPS (Training for Intervention ProcedureS) certified.

TIPS is an online skills-based, responsible alcohol training and certification program that is designed to prevent intoxication, underage drinking, and drunk driving by enhancing the fundamental "people skills" of servers, sellers, and consumers of alcohol. TIPS training gives individuals the knowledge and confidence they need to recognize potential alcohol-related problems and intervene to prevent alcohol-related tragedies.

> Requirements and regulations vary from state to state. Learn more here: www.tipsalcohol.com/

Auto Coverage

Your employees might be the safest drivers –
but they still have to contend with other drivers on the
road. An accident could lead to another person getting
injured or your vehicle getting totaled.

It happened to us. An employee was coming
back from an event and was run off the road on the
highway by a driver making a last-minute decision to
get off at the exit. The sideswipe forced our employee
into the barrier, and he hit so hard that all airbags in
the vehicle deployed. We couldn't believe anyone
came out of that vehicle uninjured. Truly, we were
lucky. Vehicles can be replaced; lives can't.

Company-owned vehicles must be covered by
commercial auto insurance. State regulations
determine how much coverage you need.

Commercial auto insurance helps cover the cost
of potential lawsuits, property damage, medical bills,
and other expenses arising from an accident. It also
pays for repairs from damage due to theft, weather
events, and vandalism.

Again, we're Cups to Gallons specialists not
insurance agents. Always make sure you have the
correct insurance in place for your business needs.

And with the nuts and bolts of those two aspects
of running a catering business covered, let's move on.

Craft the Perfect Menu – Focus on the Number "3"

Planning your catering menu is very different than the menu you have in your store.

It's unrealistic to think you'll be able to offer everything you have in your store with catering. And truly you don't want to, especially since you won't be able to bring your whole shop, equipment and all, with you.

When developing your catering menu and packages, focus on the number three.

The number three is at the heart of your catering menu's success formula. It's about giving your clients enough options, while still optimizing your profit potential with a "good, better, best" marketing strategy. By offering a low-priced, mid-priced, and high-priced catering package, you appeal to the three types of catering buyers.

Psychologically, you have three types of catering buyers. Some people are shopping on price, so the low-priced package is perfect for them. On the opposite end of the spectrum are the big spenders. They are all about ego and perception. They want the best and price is not a determining factor. Most catering clients like to play it safe and will choose the mid-priced package.

When we started with catering, we only had one option. It was basically coffee catering or smoothie catering with one size cup. Over time, we realized people wanted other options, such as longer serving time, alcohol service, larger cups, etc. As we started adding these additional options, we noticed that a third of the people ended up upgrading to the more expensive package. This was almost straight profit to the bottom line since there was nominal cost in those upgrades.

> Remember the number "3" and the number "6" regarding your menu.

By having the three packages – the good, better, and best – you attract each type of buyer. By having a low-priced catering package in the mix, you get your catering phone ringing. We always present the mid-range option first, and then based on what they say, we will tweak our sales script whether they're ultimately looking to buy based on price or if they want more options and are willing to pay for it.

Now that you know how the number "3" can help you go from cups to gallons, you need to know another number: 6

What does the number "6" have to do with catering?

Six simple words that will maximize your profits: *"Would you like fries with that?"*

Now we're not suggesting you offer fries with your catering services. What we are suggesting is that you have an upsell to what you offer. Keep to the basic packages of "good, better, and best" so that it's easy for someone to say "yes," and then once they do, you can easily ask, "Would you like _____ with that?" (fill in the blank with an upsell)

Upsells could include:

- Additional serving time
- Alcohol service (make sure you have insurance for this)
- Decorations
- Music
- Special cups
- Food items

By asking these six simple words every time you're talking with a catering prospect, you'll maximize your profits and make the client happy because they'll feel they're getting a customized package specific to their needs, thus making it easy for them to say "yes."

Ring, Ring, Ring

Once you start implementing the CATER marketing system, your phone will start ringing. Emails will come in. People will contact you wanting to know more about your catering services.

You need to be ready by having your sales scripts in place and knowing what questions to ask (or for your staff to ask), so you can present the best catering package(s) for each prospect.

Of course, the person inquiring is going to ask about price, but that is the last piece of information you'll share. *Never start a conversation with price!*

Start the conversation by qualifying the prospect. Get some basic information such as:

- Their name
- Their phone number
- Their email
- The date of the event
- The location of the event
- The number of guests
- The type of event they're planning
- The type(s) of services in which they may be interested

Should you ask about budget? No. When you follow the CATER marketing system, people will be clamoring to work with you and it won't be based on price. Never assume what someone will pay for your services.

We have three main ways people contact us:

- They fill out a "contact us" form on our website
- They call us
- They email us

You'll want to have a process in place to manage these incoming leads, to ensure they're acknowledged immediately, to provide the information they're looking for, and to move them through your sales funnel to becoming a paying (and returning) catering client.

We use a CRM (customer relationship management) system to manage our own catering processes as well as for the clients who work with us with our done-for-you marketing services.

What's a CRM? It's a super-charged database that manages all of your relationships and interactions with customers and potential customers. A good CRM can be invaluable to your business. It will keep your contacts organized and allow you to manage everything in one system. Imagine being able to look up a record in your database and know everything you need to know, a "diary" of every communication, while also providing demographics, trends, and forecasts, so you can make good business decisions, all at your fingertips:

> A good CRM system can streamline your operation and save a lot of time.

- What type of contact is it? A prospect? A client? A past client?
- What services are they interested in? What services have they used in the past?
- Who do you need to follow up with for various reasons (close a contract, finalize details, etc.)?

- What communications happened in the past? What communications need to happen next? (e.g., call, email, thank you note, etc.)
- How much revenue will you make today, tomorrow, next month?
- What is in your pipeline?
- What niche of catering is our best seller? Which is most profitable?
- Where does our catering business come from? What marketing is working best to bring in new business?

The CRM we use internally and to manage our clients' catering businesses is Infusionsoft. We've customized it to our catering needs and have all of the marketing campaigns and automations built out, so the CRM is really doing all of the heavy lifting. Each day when we log in, we know exactly what needs to be done.

You don't have to have a CRM to manage your catering activities. You can absolutely do it with a few extra manual steps and tracking. We did it manually for years using Constant Contact for our email marketing solution, Google Docs, Google Sheets, and Google Calendar to manage the day-to-day activities, scheduling, and tracking the status and sales of catering jobs.

Our CRM is integrated with our website, so when someone fills out a "Contact Us" form, that data is automatically input into the system and based on the type of catering they noted they were interested in (e.g., smoothie catering), that prospect is then automatically dropped into the appropriate marketing automation campaign.

When someone calls in, our staff inputs the contact and catering requested information directly into the CRM as well. You can absolutely do this manually. Have forms by the phone that staff completes for every catering prospect. You'll want to set up a protocol for how those are handled. Do they give the form to you? Do they input it into your database or CRM? The last thing you want to find out about later is a potential $5,000 catering job you lost because you never even knew about the lead.

What will make your catering business work seamlessly is having a *system* in place for everyone to follow. This way when there's someone new who comes on board, they just follow the system. Document what your procedures are for incoming leads for all incoming sources (e.g., website, phone, email).

Sales Scripting

When someone contacts us, the first thing we do is determine the type of catering they're looking for and the date/time of their event. We incorporate sales scripting using "scarcity" to instill a little fear that if they don't quickly reserve their event now, the date/time may not be available. We say, "Our calendar fills up this time of year. Let me check the calendar to see if we have availability on _____ (date)." Even if our calendar is completely open, we always use this sales scripting. It works and gets tire kickers to make a decision and finalize their event.

We have a very short two- to three-sentence description of each type of catering service we offer. It's memorized and is relayed the same way each and every time. That's because it works. It's all based on providing the customer what *they* want... an experience... not a cup of coffee, a smoothie, or a dessert.

It's critical you get your sales scripting perfected. When you do, you won't have to sell your catering services. They'll sell themselves.

It's Time to Cater

If you've been following the CATER system so far, you've committed to "taking your business to the people" with off-premise catering, you've defined who you're going to offer your catering services to, and you have a marketing plan to bring in new leads. You've created your catering packages, your pricing, your menus, and your phone is ringing with inquiries. You're getting catering jobs. Exciting! Now what?

You need:

- A process to manage new catering jobs – from scheduling to confirmation to payment.
- Equipment to do the job.

- A process to ensure that every job is maximized for success – the right amount of product, staffing, packing, logistics, etc.

Basically the "meat and potatoes" of catering. Get your highlighter ready. There's a lot to cover!

Someone Wants You to Cater – Now What?

When someone says, "YES! I want you to cater my event," you need to able to follow a process that is systematic, repeatable, and easy to follow. That's what the CATER system gives you. This ensures that nothing gets missed, nothing is forgotten, and you're prepared for equipment, product, and staffing.

Missing a catering job because you forgot to schedule it – BAD!

Double booking a catering job and not being able to handle it – BAD!

Showing up late for a catering job – BAD!

Not sending enough staff to handle the job – BAD!

Sending too many staff for the job – BAD!

Having a client "think" they're getting one thing, but you provide something else – BAD!

These are just a few of the bad things that can happen if you don't have the tools and templates in place to go from cups to gallons. Let's dig in so you can get it all in place and master the "T" in the CATER system.

Staffing/Scheduling

The first thing you want to do is make sure you have the date/time available to do the catering job and staff available to do the job. We use Google Calendar to keep track of all catering jobs. This makes it easy for everyone to see it from any device.

Our catering jobs are based on a two-hour serving window. Clients can pay for additional time if they wish, but most jobs are two hours. That's just for the service itself. You need to build in time for packing, driving, unloading, setup, tear down, driving back, and unpacking.

We always get to a job at least 30 minutes before serving time. We now have it down pat for unloading and setting up. As you're getting started, you may want to add additional setup time. A client never complains that you're there early. They do complain when you're late. You don't want to make your client stressed or unhappy right before their event because you're not able to start serving when you said you would.

> Allow enough time to pack up, drive to the location, and setup. It's always better to be too early.

Working backward, if a catering job were scheduled from 1:00 – 3:00 p.m., staff would start packing up at 11:00 a.m. (two hours before the start of the event). This gives them a half hour to grab supplies and pack up. They leave for the event at 11:30, giving them an hour to get to the location. (Most of our events are within 30 minutes thus giving a 30-minute buffer "in case," and staff is required to check for traffic before they leave, so they know how much time it will take them to get there and they're not stressed driving like a maniac to arrive on time). Again, always plan ahead. Accidents will happen. Traffic will be snarled. Give yourself and/or your staff plenty of time to get there, unload, and setup, so they're not stressed and rushed. A calm caterer equals a happy host/hostess.

When the event is over, it takes about 30 minutes to tear down and load up the vehicle. Then about 30 minutes to get back and unpack.

In summary, if a catering event is scheduled from 1:00 – 3:00 p.m., we would block off 11:00 a.m. – 5:00 p.m. on the calendar.

How many people do you need for each catering job? We know that one person can serve up to 75 guests in a two-hour timeframe for both coffee and/or smoothie catering. If the event is larger, we add an additional staff person. Sometimes the client will specifically request an additional server for the two-hour window. We charge extra for that time.

You'll also want to make sure you have enough vehicles and equipment to handle the catering jobs being booked each day. We're able to handle three jobs simultaneously, which could be a combination of two coffee and/or two smoothie jobs at the same time.

It's important to look at your calendar when someone is looking to book a job and/or says "yes" to booking a job to ensure you have the availability to do it. When someone hasn't yet said "yes" but is looking for a quote and/or getting information, we will "pencil" them in the calendar by putting a question mark before the name of the event so that they get first right of refusal. If another potential client contacts us wanting the same date and time, we will reach out to the first contact, letting them know someone else is interested in booking and that we need a commitment. Since they had contacted us first, we're giving them the first right of refusal.

That's a great problem to have: too many jobs for the same day and time. It happens to us as well. When we see that we're already fully booked for a particular day/time the client is looking for, we'll ask if they have any flexibility to do it at another day/time. Most clients do and we're able to accommodate them.

> Scarcity sells. Allude to a full calendar when speaking with prospects.

We've actually been able to train our clients to reach out to us further in advance to ensure they get their preferred date and time because they know how full our schedule is, especially during certain times of the year such as Teacher Appreciation Week and other popular holidays during the year.

Secret hint: Even if your calendar isn't full, you can position it that it is by saying to potential clients, "Our calendar is very full that day. I think I can fit one more job on the schedule. Would you like to finalize the details?" That gets them committed and positions it that you're very popular and busy, so they better book now or it may not be available later.

Critical Information & Contracts

When someone says "YES! I want you to cater my event," you want to get at a minimum the following information:

- Date of event
- Time of event
- Address of event
- Type of service being provided
- Number of people to serve
- Contact person for day of event

We have a template that we use to add all of this information. It is the basis of the contract that we create.

Speaking of contracts…

You definitely want one, but it doesn't have to be a long, complicated, overly legalese-worded document. Ours is a simple one-page document that lays out the basics of the services to be provided. Basically everything noted above. We send the contract to the client via DocuSign that makes it very simple for them to "sign" and return. We then have an electronic copy of it for our records.

Some of the boiler-plate information that is included in every contract includes payment types (cash, credit cards, checks), gratuity information, cancellation policy (and potential penalty fee), and alcohol guidelines as needed.

The week of the upcoming catering event, we send out a confirmation/reminder email that we're excited to be providing (type of catering service) at (time of event), who their server will be, and if there's a balance on their account. Clients appreciate getting these confirmations and it shows your professionalism as a caterer.

Equipment

Now that you have the pieces in place regarding what to do before the catering event, let's talk about what you need in order to do the catering job – equipment.

Wouldn't it be great it you could just take your brick-and-mortar location with you, so you have everything you need to do a catering job? Obviously you can't do that, so you need to have the right equipment.

Everything you'll need will have to be mobile/portable and fit into one vehicle. We pack everything into heavy-duty tubs and every vehicle has a commercial-grade hand cart. This makes it easy to roll in and roll out.

The specific equipment you need to do catering will vary based on what you're doing and the experience you want to provide. For smoothie catering, we have a portable tiki bar. For coffee catering, we serve from black draped tables. You'll need to determine what your setup will be. The ancillary supplies needed will vary as well based on the type of catering. Smoothie catering requires a blender, blender tops, ice, smoothie mix, cups, straws, etc. Coffee catering requires its own equipment and supplies.

Since many of those reading this book are coffee shops, we asked Joe Kolb, owner of Espresso Outlet to contribute what to consider when selecting coffee catering equipment.

Espresso Machine

Espresso-based drinks such as lattes and cappuccinos make up a significant percentage of drinks consumed by a typical coffee drinker, so it is obviously the most important piece of equipment to get right. If you get a machine that is too large, it will make it difficult to transport and move around. If you get a machine that is too small, you will have a hard time keeping up with making drinks and the drink quality will be poor due to wide fluctuations in temperature that have an adverse effect on the flavor of espresso shots. It is usually ideal to have a single-group machine with as large of a boiler as possible or a compact two-group machine.

Another important espresso machine factor to consider is the type of electrical connection the machine has. For many on-site catering events, it tends to be easiest to have access to 120-volt outlets vs 220-volt outlets, so in most cases, it is best to have a 120-volt machine. The drawback is you can't make as many drinks per hour on a 120-volt machine, but the benefit of having a suitable outlet available tends to outweigh this drawback.

Espresso machines require a source of water for operation, which is used for brewing espresso and steaming milk. There are a few light commercial machines that have built in water tanks, but constantly filling a water tank during service can be a hassle, especially during a rush. For this reason, it is usually best to have a machine that has a direct water line connection and to connect it to a five-gallon water tank using a pump called a Flojet.

Ease of use is another thing to keep in mind when choosing an espresso machine. It is important to get a machine that is as easy to use as possible without sacrificing the quality of the drinks produced. We recommend traditional pump espresso machines that have volumetric dosing for the shot volumes, but we don't recommend super automatics. Super automatic machines are the easiest to use, but they tend to produce subpar drinks. Super automatic machines also tend to cost a lot more than other machine types and tend to require more maintenance and cleaning.

> Keep portability and electrical requirements in mind when choosing equipment.

Many health departments have rules that require espresso machines and grinders to have safety ratings, such as NSF, so keep this in mind when purchasing equipment for your catering service.

There are a range of other factors to consider, but these are the most important ones.

Grinders

While some espresso machines can be used with espresso pods, for best brewing results, it is highly recommended to always use freshly ground coffee. In terms of impact on flavor, a grinder can have more impact on flavor than the espresso machine, so choosing a grinder shouldn't be an afterthought. If your service offers more than just espresso, such as pour overs, then you may need more than one grinder. A grinder that is ideal for catering is one that is fast, doesn't overheat, is easily adjusted, and lightweight.

Batch-Brewed Coffee

Regular drip or batch-brewed coffee is a good item to have available. If the event is close enough to your location, you may be able to brew a few airpots before your catering event, but there are times when it is beneficial to have a brewer available, especially for larger catering events or events that last longer. Due to the size of batch brewers, it is best to get smaller units for better portability, and as with espresso machines, it is easier to get access to 120-volt connections, so brewers with that kind of connection are usually a good idea. If you have several airpots, you can have some pre-brewed before the start of service.

If it is not ideal to bring separate brewing equipment, such as at small events, you can always use the espresso machine to brew Americanos. Just make sure you get an espresso machine that has a hot water spigot, so you can add six ounces of hot water to a double shot of espresso.

Accessories

You will need a variety of accessory items to make service a success. For steaming, it will be good to have at least a couple steam pitchers and microfiber cloths for wiping the steam wand after use. It is also ideal to have a cold water rinser to clean the pitcher quickly between uses.

For brewing, you will need a couple tampers and a knockbox. It is also beneficial to have a brush for cleaning the group periodically during use, as well as microfibers cloths for wiping out the filter basket from time to time.

Equipment Maintenance

Basic maintenance can go a long way in preserving the life of your equipment. Preventing limescale buildup in your machine can prevent a myriad of issues that can be caused by calcium buildup on internal components. Always use soft water that is less than 50 ppm in hardness, but more than zero (such as distilled water). Even with soft water, it is a good idea to descale the machine after several months of use. At the end of each use, backflushing the grouphead will get rid of coffee residue. This will prevent the grouphead from getting gummed up with coffee oils and ensure that your drinks don't start getting a rancid flavor.

For grinders, it is a good idea to use grinder cleaning tablets every few weeks to remove coffee oil from the burrs to ensure that the grind quality remains as high as possible. When you do this, it also a good idea to vacuum out the grind chamber and use a stiff brush to break up any buildup in the chamber.

Other Non-Coffee Equipment

Hey smoothie, juice, ice cream, dessert and snack shop owners: We didn't forget about you!

The equipment that you need to do catering will obviously vary depending on the type of catering you do. Obviously, coffee catering needs coffee equipment. Smoothie catering needs smoothie equipment, etc. We could write an entire book just on equipment for each of the different types of businesses that want to go from cups to gallons. Don't worry!

We're very happy to help. Just send us an email to cupstogallonssuccess@gmail.com, and we'll answer all of your questions and help you determine what equipment is needed for the type of catering you'll be doing.

Checklists

What makes the "T" in the CATER system work is having systems in place. Use checklists to ensure that everything you need is packed. Build out and document your process from the moment someone contacts you to learn more through the moment your staff returns. This way it becomes a wash, lather, rinse, repeat exercise. Doing this has allowed us to build a business that doesn't rely on us.

With processes documented and checklists in place, everyone knows what to do, how to do it, and when to do it. The result is a consistent, excellent experience for every client, and that goes a long way to building your reputation, increasing efficiency, and boosting your bottom line.

Cups to Gallons, Pennies to Dollars:

- Understanding health department requirements and insurance needs are the first step in building a successful business. Overlooking either of these can lead to disaster.
- Craft the perfect menu by focusing on "3": good, better, best offerings.
- Upsell!
- Have a script ready for incoming calls and never, ever start with price.
- A good CRM system can streamline your operation and save a lot of time; however, when you're starting out, you can set up simple, manual systems.
- Your sales script should suggest scarcity, "Let me check our calendar to see if that date is open."

- Ensure enough time on the calendar for a catering job, including packing, transportation, setup, service, and cleaning up.
- You'll need portable equipment, but there are many considerations besides portability including electrical requirements and service size.
- Have a process to manage every catering job from confirmation to payment... and document it. Consider joining our Cups to Gallons Catering Training Program.

The Cups To Gallons Training Program goes into detail on every aspect of catering, including giving you the exact tools and templates we use in our catering business. Learn more: CupsToGallons.com/training

Chapter Eight

E xperience

Most new caterers think the food or the drink is the most important thing. WRONG!

The "E" in the CATER system is all about the experience. Get this right and you'll be able to charge premiums prices without any resistance while having customers coming back again and again with open wallets.

Catering is a commodity. People can get it anywhere. They can pick up a box of coffee on the way to the office. They can have a box of coffee dropped off at the office. Remember the "C" in the CATER system?

It's about changing the business model and going *to* the people. When you do that and provide a done-for-you solution, people will pay handsomely for it. You deliver on that by providing an experience.

Think of Disney theme parks. One ticket is over $100 while most other theme park ticket prices range between $25 - $60. Yet Disney parks are full every day, and their attendance continues to grow with average guest spending increasing by four percent (See the Resource section for links to the statistics.) They actually *raise* the price on days when they know they're especially busy.

Have you been to Disney? Probably more than once. And it wasn't just the park ticket you paid for.

It's the travel to get there, lodging, meals, and Mickey Mouse souvenirs, of course. We've never heard anyone complain about how much money they spent. That's because they loved it! It was an experience that anyone who's been there can still talk about to this day.

Everything at Disney is based on delivering an experience. There are many ways they do this, many of which visitors probably don't actually recognize. Disney calls their employees cast members. The parks are remarkably clean – bathrooms are pristine, rarely do you see gum on the ground, no bugs, trash cans are never more than a few yards away. And that's just scratching the surface of the details that Disney orchestrates to ensure it's the "happiest and most magical place on earth."

> You're not just catering an event. You're creating an experience!

With your catering, the experience starts from the moment someone is searching for what you offer to what follow-up procedures you have in place so they're excited to leave reviews, refer others, and come back again.

Think of the experience you're trying to create as a "story"… from "once up on a time" until "the end," how do you want people to feel along the journey? How can you ensure it's delightful for them?

The experience needs to align with your branding or theme. Customer expectations are based on your brand promise. What level of catering services will you deliver?

If your concept is based on an elaborate black-tie experience, then you need to deliver an experience that's similar. Our theme is "tropical," so customers are not expecting drinks to be served from high-priced china. They're totally okay with us serving from plastic disposable cups.

Here are a few ways we deliver an experience:

- We answer the phone, "Aloha!"
- The font we use in our emails is "tropical."
- The names of our catering packages have "tropical names."
- We call our staff "tikitenders."
- We don't do "catering" – we provide The Ultimate Hawaiian Getaway Without a 12-Hour Flight.
- Staff wears bright floral Hawaiian shirts.
- Drinks are blended fresh, made to order, and topped off with a Hawaiian parasol.
- We don't call our drinks "smoothies" – we call them a "vacation in a cup!"

Nothing above says anything about "We have the best-tasting products in the world!" From the moment someone reaches out to us to learn about our catering services, they're brought into the story – the story of how we'll bring Hawaii to them and their guests. They'll be so happy, everyone will be doing the hula. They're not buying on price. *They're buying the EXPERIENCE.*

Your experience should include at a minimum:

- Confirming details of the event before you arrive, so there are no misunderstandings – what you're providing, how many people, if there's a balance due, etc.
- Making sure your staff shows up early, smiling, ready to deliver an amazing experience to the guests.
- Ensuring your equipment is pristine – if you have a dirty blender or coffee maker, they may question the quality of your product.
- Ensuring your vehicle is clean inside and out.

Presentation, Presentation, Presentation

In retail, it's about location, location, location. In catering it's about presentation, presentation, presentation. After all, what is an amazing tasting coffee, smoothie, juice, ice cream, dessert or snack if you can't have a little fun with it? If you really want to impress your catering clients, make it memorable for them. From the equipment to the menu to how you serve – it all tells a story that creates your experience.

We serve smoothies from a tiki bar. When guests see it from a distance, they're already smiling and saying, "What a cool tiki bar!" Now if we were serving from a regular table, they probably wouldn't have that reaction. We have tropical music playing in the background. Our staff wears bright Hawaiian shirts and greets guests with, "Aloha!" Our menu features tropical drink names, and sometimes we even customize the menu to our client's theme. We'll have signature drinks that relate to the name of the client, their colors and/or their theme. We can provide leis to guests (an additional add-on). We make everything fresh on-site to order. And we top every beverage off with a Hawaiian parasol. Again, we don't call our smoothies smoothies; we call them a "Vacation in a cup!" We don't call our catering catering; we call it "The Ultimate Hawaiian Getaway Without a 12-Hour Flight." Now that's an experience!

Think of all of the moving parts of your "catering story" and build out an experience that is enjoyable for both you and your guests, so it's an event everyone remembers. Remember, when you sell an experience, no one questions the price.

A common question we're asked is, "Should we use our own branded cups when catering?" Absolutely not! While everything in your store is probably about *your* brand – the cups, the napkins, etc. – when you do catering, you want to keep it all generic. It's not about promoting your business – it's about delivering an experience that delights the guests. Delighted guests make delighted hosts/hostesses.

When they say, "Wow!" you've greased the skids to fulfill the final piece of the CATER system. When they say, "Wow!" price will never be a factor. Remember what we covered earlier: People can buy what they *need* anywhere, but they will happily pay a premium price for what they *want*. Deliver the experience they want!

Cups to Gallons, Pennies to Dollars:

- Keep the Disney approach in mind. Their ticket prices are noticeably higher than others, but guest spending continues to increase. People are willing to pay for the experience.
- Start building your prospect's experience from the moment they first contact you.
- Your experience is a story. From "once upon a time" until "the end," how do you want your clients to feel? How can you delight them?
- However you brand your business and the experience you deliver, carry that through everything you do, like our example that starts with "Aloha!"
- It's all about presentation, presentation, presentation when it comes to catering.

Want to learn more about how to create an EXPERIENCE with your catering? "Small Business Stacey" shares her top videos and content on how to do it step-by-step.
Grab it here: CupsToGallons.com/experience

Chapter Nine:

Ratings, Reviews & Reputation

It doesn't matter what you say about yourself. What others say about you is what matters, especially when it comes to your catering.

Of course, you can say you have the best products, the best service, the best catering in town. But that's just chest beating. Every one of your competitors can say that also. What will help you get more catering clients is ensuring you have a good reputation – online and offline… because people *will* check you out.

They'll check out review sites; they'll ask about you on social media; they'll even ask you for references. Make sure you're proud of your reputation.

After you've delivered a "Wow!" experience, make sure you have a process to get testimonials after every catering job. Your host/hostess will never be happier than at the end of their event when everyone has been commending them for the great experience provided. This is the best time to ask!

What we don't recommend, however, is bothering them to get a review immediately upon the conclusion of the event. They're busy entertaining. The last thing they want is to have a tablet shoved in their face asking, "Will you leave me a review?"

We prep the host/hostess before the event even begins by noting in their confirmation email that we "want to leave them so happy, they'll be doing the hula," and if we do, the biggest compliment they can give is a review or testimonial. Works like a charm!

Of course, they have a fantastic event and are thrilled with the great-tasting beverages and amazing service. We've helped make them look like the "host/hostess with the mostess" to their guests and they're overjoyed we made it so easy for them. Here's how we conclude the event: As the server is leaving, they mention to the client that they'll be getting an email the next day and they'd appreciate if they would leave a positive review.

> Ratings and referrals make your next sale easier. Always ask for them... at the right time.

We use a tool called Reputation Stacker that automates the review process. It sends out the email after each catering job and allows the person to give a rating (up to five stars) and then post on the appropriate social channel of their choice where they'd like their review to be posted. We found this works better than asking for a review right after the event as many times the host/hostess is still entertaining and/or busy. Because each of the review sites requires a log in, we found people were not comfortable putting their credentials into our tablets.

Let's look at things to consider as you're setting up your reputation management process.

Sites to Consider

Here are the sites that will have the biggest impact on your online reputation, both for getting found in search and those that people use most:

- Google/Google My Business
- Yelp
- Facebook

Google/Google My Business

A presence on this platform is a must for your business. Google is the biggest search engine in the world. They want their visitors to have a good experience in using their site, so showing reviews and ratings allows their visitors to make informed decisions.

Make sure you setup and/or claim your Google My Business profile (www.google.com/business). Here you'll be able to upload photos from catering events, post helpful content such as Q&As, or timely ideas for catering such as "5 Ways to Improve Staff Morale During Stressful Tax Season." You'll also get valuable analytics that show you how people are finding you online and what content they're engaging with most.

Yelp

Most people in the restaurant and/or catering industry think of Yelp as a four-letter word. We agree, but it is a necessary evil.

Ensuring you're getting positive reviews on Yelp does matter. Here's why:

- In one Harvard Business School study, just a one-star increase in a Yelp rating leads to a five- to nine-percent increase in revenue for independent restaurants.
- 72% of consumers say that positive reviews make them trust a local business more.
- A study by UC Berkeley economists found that just a half-star increase on Yelp translates to a 19% greater likelihood that a restaurant will be full during peak dining times.
- According to ReviewTrackers' 2018 Online Review Survey, 45% of consumers say they're likely to check Yelp reviews before visiting a business. *That's second only to Google (64%)!*

With a monthly average of more than 178 million unique visitors, Yelp has become the go-to resource for crowdsourced reviews about local restaurants and catering businesses. And people really trust the ratings they find. (See the Resource section for the link to the studies.)

Here are the steps you'll want to take to market your business on Yelp:

1. Claim your Yelp business page https://biz.yelp.com.
2. Review your business information – ensure everything is correct.
3. Read and respond to customer reviews – yes even the negative ones.
4. Post photos showcasing your catering services.
5. Offer specials deals and/or gift certificates.
6. Track analytics.
7. Promote your business listing by adding the Yelp badge to your website, email signature, and email newsletters.

A common question we're asked is "Should I advertise on Yelp?" We advise our clients to put their marketing dollars elsewhere in promoting their catering services. We've had much better success with Google AdWords. Yelp will run your ads under generic terms like "catering," so they can say they're getting you a lot of impressions, but catering is way too generic (and expensive) when you're only specializing in a type of catering – coffee, smoothie, juice bar, etc. Also, Yelp ads do not send traffic to your website, so you're losing a huge opportunity to drive leads and educate prospective catering clients about your services. Make your own informed decision, but in general, we have found our clients do much better with their marketing dollars being spent elsewhere.

Facebook

Facebook now has over 2.7 billion users. It's where your customers are. A whopping 88 percent of people trust what friends and even strangers say on Facebook about businesses. Whether someone shares the beverage they just got from your most recent catering job or your client posts a review of the service, these Facebook mentions matter.

Facebook star ratings appear in the search results in Google, so don't forget to utilize this important platform for your reviews.

On your Facebook page, go to your settings and make sure you've set it to allow people to write reviews on Facebook.

Other Review Sites to Consider

There are many niche-specific review sites on which you may want to consider setting up a profile and actively managing your reputation:

- Wedding Wire
- The Knot
- Gig Salad
- Partypop.com
- Gatheringuide.com

- Localcatering.com

Manage Your Local Listings

Search engines like Google analyze your business location. Search results for catering services in your area are partially dictated by businesses Google *knows are nearby*.

Your business information is aggregated (address, contact information) from many online resources for consistency purposes.

Your online listings must have precisely the same information – even slight variations cause issues. Make sure that basic information (address, phone number, hours of operation) are updated and correct across all listings. Incorrect or misleading data is more than enough to convince any consumer to look for other options.

Monitor and Respond to Reviews

People will be checking you out online to see what others are saying about your catering services, so it's important to monitor and respond to reviews to further shape your online presence.

When prospective catering clients see that you're engaging and responding to reviews, it lets them know you care about providing great service. Thanking someone for posting a positive review is great, but it's even more important to respond to negative feedback. By crafting a well-written and on-brand response, you show the reviewer and potential catering clients that you care about the feedback and use the pain points brought up in the review to improve the experience.

The "Don'ts" of Dealing with Negative Online Reviews

If a customer called up your company to talk about the service they received, you wouldn't ignore their call or listen and hang up without saying anything. The same goes for online reviews.

If you get a bad review, here is how *not* to go about dealing with the situation.

Don't Get Defensive

It's natural to get mad when someone criticizes your business, especially if you feel the complaint is unfounded. You care about your business; you care about your catering clients, so a bad review can feel like an attack.

But responding in anger does no good — and might possibly spiral into a viral nightmare. When you see a negative review, don't respond immediately. Take some time to get your thoughts in order before responding. Maybe even write your response in an email to yourself to see how your thoughts come across on screen.

If you feel as though the situation was a total miscommunication, it might be hard to sound genuinely apologetic and *not* defensive. Even if you were in the right, try not to rub that in the customer's face—it'll only make the situation worse.

Don't Ignore It

Ignoring a negative online review is almost as bad as posting an expletive-filled answer. First, the reviewer will feel completely justified in their anger because you're not addressing the issue.

Second, others will start to wonder if you really care or if they can expect the same brush-off if they have a bad experience.

Being unresponsive on a bad review might signal to current and future customers that you really *don't* care about customer service, and situations like these aren't all that uncommon for your business.

Don't Get Pulled into an Online Battle

No matter how polite your initial response, you may run into a troll who just wants to keep complaining online.

If your interaction threatens to escalate into an exchange of name-calling, simply re-state that you're happy to resolve the issue and ask the person to contact you offline. Other readers will see that you're being reasonable and that the troll isn't. But if you engage with someone who just wants to pick a fight, other quality catering clients might think you're just as petty as the complainer.

Don't Beg for Positive Reviews to Hide the Negative Ones

If you happen to get a negative review, your first inclination may be to beg customers to give you positive ones.

The best reviews for your business are those written by customers who were naturally compelled to gush about how great your catering services are. So if you have to pull teeth to get people to say great things about you, it won't sound genuine on your review pages. And if you are asking for reviews to hide negative ones, customers will know what's up. If there are a bunch of fake-sounding positive reviews scattered between genuinely negative ones, odds are people reading them will take the negative ones to heart.

The "Do's" of Dealing with Negative Online Reviews

Now you know what to avoid when it comes to online reviews — that's the easy part.

So here's what you *should* do when confronted with a negative online review.

Acknowledge the Issue and Apologize

Just like in real life, most people who complain on the internet simply want to be heard. Before you try to get to the bottom of the problem, it's crucial to empathize with them and apologize without blaming them. Show that you genuinely regret that a catering client didn't have the experience they expected.

And when you do apologize and explain the issue, you might change a customer's mind and turn the negative into a positive!

Tactfully Promote a Positive Image of Your Business

Without sounding like you're contradicting the reviewer, convey why their experience is rare in sincere and non-condescending language.

If it feels natural, include some of your catering strengths in your reply. Responses can be a great way to flip the script and frame your business in a positive light — while still making the customer feel heard.

Be Authentic and Personal

You never want to come off like you're giving a canned response. When responding to negative online reviews, use your real name (or first name and last initial), explain your role in the business, and give your direct phone number or email.

When it comes to replying to negative reviews, sincerity is the key. The easiest way to be authentic is to reach out to the reviewer on a personal level.

Take It Offline

To avoid an online exchange that everyone can see, you should always strive to leave a sincere, thought-out public comment and *then* take the discussion of the issue offline.

Here's an example of how to respond to a negative online review:

"This is Stacey Riska, owner of Maui Wowi Hawaiian Coffees & Smoothies [authentic and personal]. I'm sorry you were unhappy with the service you received at your catering event [clearly states facts without blame]. Our goal is for every catering client to have an event that leaves them thrilled with the experience [promotes positive image]. Please call or email me at [contact information] so I can resolve this issue to your satisfaction."

If it feels right, taking the issue offline shows that you're fully willing to handle this situation—and you're not just apologizing for show.

The Biggest "Do" of All

Once you've dealt with the situation appropriately, *do* use negative reviews as a learning experience.

If you consistently receive negative reviews or if a lot of reviews cite the same criticism—such as a poor server or bad-tasting drinks—something's up. This isn't just a one-off blip.

Consistently negative reviews mean that it's time to make a change. Consider it free market research!

Set Up Google Alerts for Your Business

Wouldn't it be great if you could be notified when someone is saying something about your business or a specific keyword you're interested in (e.g., coffee catering)? You can!

The Google Alerts tool lets you add keywords related to your business, so whenever online news comes up about your business, you see it.

Leverage Your Positive Reviews

When you get a great review, reach out to the customer to ask for permission to use it in marketing materials. If you get permission, you can use it in many ways:

Share Your Reviews on Social Media

Whether your catering clients express it in video, audio, or written form, these customer reviews can easily be shared on your social media channels. Enhancing it with photographs from their event gives prospective clients an idea of what your catering services are like.

We tag our clients when we reshare their reviews. This lets them know we appreciate them, and in many cases, they'll then share and repost the review giving us additional visibility and exposure.

Add Reviews on Your Business Cards

This can be very powerful especially if you get a review from a well-known publication, food critic, or local celebrity. Business cards are easily passed around between prospects and existing catering clients who will gladly make referrals.

Incorporate Reviews on Your Website

There's a right way and a wrong way to use reviews on your website. You don't want to come across as chest beating, arrogant, or boastful. The goal is to show third-party credence while balancing the integrity of each review so it seems genuine and not manufactured.

We put a few name-worthy testimonials on the front page of our website along with their company logos. Because we use Reputation Stacker as our reputation management tool, it allows us to feed in those reviews directly to our site as well. This helps to immediately establish credibility. We also have a page on our site dedicated to showcasing all client testimonials, so anyone can easily scroll through and see the many events we've done.

Post Reviews in Your Store

Create a "wall of fame" and share all of the testimonials and positive reviews you've received. They serve as positive reinforcement and encouragement to your team, as well as contributing to a client-focused culture. And of course, they'll be a reminder to those in your store that you do a great job with catering.

Feature Reviews in Your Email Newsletters

Sharing reviews from previous catering jobs in your emails reinforces the great experiences you provide. It can also incentivize clients to leave reviews. Don't forget to include a link to the main review sites to make it easy for them to leave you a review.

Highlight Reviews in Proposals/Quotes

When you're at the point of presenting a proposal, positive reviews can help close the deal by demonstrating your excellence. This can help ensure that clients don't get cold feet right before making a commitment to work with your catering company on their event.

Research Your Online Reviews

Search for your online reviews and see what people are saying about you. This is valuable insight on how your catering business is doing and where you may need to improve.

Reviews and sentiment really do impact your business.

What people say about your business can determine its success. Take reviews about your company and catering services seriously. When it's negative, you can take steps to rectify the situation and possibly garner more positive press for your business. When it's positive, recognize and thank reviewers for taking the time to praise your business.

Cups to Gallons, Pennies to Dollars:

- Create a process to ask for a rating/review after the event but not immediately upon its conclusion.
- Some sites have a bigger impact on your online reputation, including Google, Yelp, and Facebook.
- Yelp is not a four-letter word. Statistics prove that ratings there can truly impact businesses, especially in the food-service industry.
- You must monitor and respond to the reviews you receive.
- The don'ts of dealing with negative online reviews are don't:
  o Get defensive
  o Ignore it
  o Get pulled into an online battle
  o Beg for positive reviews
- Here's what you should do:
  o Acknowledge and apologize

- o Tactfully promote your business's positive image
- o Be authentic and personal
- o Take it offline
- Similar negative reviews indicate there's something wrong. Take steps to fix it.
- Be sure to leverage all of your positive reviews!

Did you know there are over 400 sites where customers can write you a review – and counting! Want access to the FREE spreadsheet? Access and download it here: www.cupstogallons.com/reviewsites

Chapter Ten:

What's Next?

We want to thank you for reading this book. You have many options when it comes to how you invest your time, especially when it comes to building your business.

You now have the five steps to go from cups to gallons using the CATER system. You can put many of these ideas into action immediately

The information shared here is the exact system others pay us $5,000 a day to learn. Why then would we give it away for free? It's simple. We know 90 percent of our fellow independent coffee, smoothie, juice bar, ice cream, dessert and snack shop owners will read this book, find it interesting, even get excited... but then do nothing.

This book is really for the other 10 percent: the movers, shakers, and doers. Nothing happens until you take action. Finishing this book makes you an action taker. Congrats!

You have three options when it comes to implementing the CATER system:

- You can do it yourself
- You can do it with some help
- You can have a done-for-you solution

This book gives you the blueprint to get your catering business started. You can absolutely do it yourself. Some additional free resources you'll want to take advantage of are on the CupsToGallons.com website. There's a lot of free training and resources there, and it's constantly updated with new information.

Make sure you join the free Cups to Gallons Facebook group. This is another free resource where you can ask questions and get feedback on all of your catering efforts. There's live trainings and events in the group, and you'll meet some other great people going from cups to gallons.

Most people reading this book will realize catering is the solution you've been looking for and is a perfect and low-cost add-on to the business you've already built. Naturally, you're a bit nervous to just jump in. You'd like to have some additional training. Some hands-on support. An opportunity to get every one of your questions answered.

That's why we've created the Cups to Gallons Training Program – a live event where we teach you how to get your first – or next – catering job in the next 30 days. Just one catering job easily pays for this training. To learn more about the training program and upcoming events, go to CupsToGallons.com/CATER.

A few of those reading this book will say, "Stacey and Dave, this sounds amazing. I want the fastest results. Can you just do it for me?" Yes – and no. We do offer done-for-you marketing solutions, where we'll do the marketing to get you catering jobs. You just do the jobs. We'll help you define the niche(s) on which to focus, and we'll implement the top marketing strategies to bring in new catering clients. We can even manage the contract, confirmation, and follow-up process. This is a very concierge-level program.

To learn more, schedule a 30-minute initial Cups to Gallons consult with us at:

Calendly.com/smallbizstacey/cups-to-gallons-free-consult

You now have the exact system we used to transform our business from $500K in debt to a seven-figure profitable business. A business that took us from cups to gallons.

You can also have tremendous success by getting into lucrative catering.

So… are you ready to CATER?

What's Next?

Resources:

Chapter 3:
Join the FREE Cups To Gallons Facebook Group:
www.facebook.com/groups/CupsToGallons

Chapter 4:
Schedule Cups to Gallons Marketing Strategy Consultations at
https://calendly.com/smallbizstacey/cups-to-gallons-free-consult

Chapter 6:
Grab your free copy of
Small Business Marketing Made EZ:
https://smallbizmarketingspecialist.com/book/

Google ads
https://ads.google.com

Facebook ads
https://www.facebook.com/business

Check your site for mobile responsiveness:
https://responsivedesignchecker.com/

MailChimp
https://mailchimp.com

Constant Contact
https://www.constantcontact.com

Infusionsoft by Keap
https://keap.com/infusionsoft

Alignable
https://www.alignable.com/

Holiday information:
holidayinsights.com

Ch. 7

TIPS Training
https://www.tipsalcohol.com/

Google Docs, Google Sheets, and Google Calendar
https://docs.google.com
https://calendar.google.com

DocuSign
https://go.docusign.com

Ch. 8

Theme park statistics:
https://www.hometogo.com/media/theme-park-price-ranking/

https://econsultancy.com/how-disney-world-has-mastered-customer-experience/

Ch. 9

Reputation Stacker
https://reputationstacker.com

Google My Business
www.google.com/business

Yelp Statistics:
https://www.barqar.com/2019/05/09/how-yelp-is-changing-the-restaurant-catering-industry/

Yelp:
https://biz.yelp.com

Google AdWords:
https://ads.google.com

Google Alerts:
https://www.google.com/alerts

Resources

About the Authors

Stacey and Dave Riska own a very successful and profitable tropical-themed coffee and smoothie catering business in the Washington, D.C. area. All their days weren't bright and shiny however.

After opening up two stores in Dulles Airport, one store in a mall, ten mobile units and two food trucks, they were on the brink of collapse (and $500K in debt). What they quickly learned is a lesson they now teach other independent coffee, smoothie, juice bar, ice cream, dessert and snack shop owners: "Gross is for vanity, net is for sanity."

Instead of selling one cup of coffee or smoothie at a time, they realized the power – and profitability – of selling by the gallon and providing off-premise catering. This transformed their business from $500K in debt to a seven-figure profitable business.

Stacey Riska, aka "Small Business Stacey," is an internationally renowned small business marketing expert and serial entrepreneur. She eats, sleeps, and breathes small business and understands exactly what it takes for the small business owner in any niche or industry to not only survive but to thrive and build the business they dream of.

Her book, *Small Business Marketing Made EZ* lays out the ACTION marketing system – a simple six-step plan to grow a successful and profitable business… the same exact six steps she used to transform her coffee/smoothie business from cups to gallons.

Dave Riska, aka "Digital Dave," helps business owners leverage the power of technology to become more efficient and productive. Whether it's designing a website that converts leads into paying customers or building out sales and marketing automation funnels that "deliver the right message to the right person at the right time," Dave is a master at utilizing the right technologies to help businesses grow.

What you won't get with Dave is a lot of technobabble or techno-fluff. He's a sought-after speaker, trainer, and consultant known for making technology "fun, understandable, and actionable."

When Stacey and Dave aren't saving small business, they love traveling, visiting "Main Street" businesses, volunteering for organizations they're passionate about, and spending quality time with their two grown children.

Made in the USA
Middletown, DE
31 December 2019